CHURCH WITHOUT WALLS

CHURCH WITHOUT WALLS

Essays on the Role of the Parish in Contemporary Society

EDITED BY

BARNABAS LINDARS, s.s.f.

The Pallion Centenary Book

London   S·P·C·K   1968

First published in 1968
by S.P.C.K.
Holy Trinity Church
Marylebone Road
London, N.W.1

Made and printed in Great Britain by
William Clowes and Sons, Limited
London and Beccles

© *St. Luke's Parochial Fund*
  Pallion, Sunderland, 1968

SBN 281 02271 2

CONTENTS

Acknowledgements   vii

Contributors   ix

Preface   xi

1   Worshippers Occasional and Lapsed   1
    by Colin Hickling

2   Pastors and Parishioners   19
    by Ronald Bowlby

3   The Parish Church and the Industrial Worker   32
    by Gordon Hopkins

4   The Challenge to Authority   41
    by Michael Keeling

5   Professors, Priests, and People   63
    by Barnabas Lindars

6   The Perils of Biblical Preaching   79
    by Barnabas Lindars

7   Reading the Bible Today   93
    by Colin Hickling

8   An Approach to Teaching   117
    by Michael Keeling

9   Willingly to School   135
    by Gordon Hopkins

ACKNOWLEDGEMENTS

Thanks are due to the following for permission to quote from copyright sources:

George Allen & Unwin Ltd: *The Casework Relationship*, by Felix Biestek.

Hodder & Stoughton Ltd and The Fortress Press: *Unchanging Mission*, by Douglas Webster.

Laurence Pollinger Ltd and the Estate of the late Mrs Frieda Lawrence and the Viking Press, Inc.: *Women in Love* © 1920, 1922 by David Herbert Lawrence, 1948, 1950 by Frieda Lawrence.

S.C.M. Press Ltd and Association Press: *Worship and Mission*, by J. G. Davies.

Professor C. H. Vereker, the Chief Education Officer of the Gloucestershire County Council, and The Gloucestershire Association for Family Life: an extract from a lecture by Professor Vereker on "Moral Education in a Changing Society".

THE CONTRIBUTORS

The Reverend Ronald Dowlby is Vicar of Croydon, and was Assistant Curate at St Luke's, Pallion, 1952-6.

The Reverend Colin Hickling is Assistant Lecturer in New Testament Studies at the University of London King's College, and was Assistant Curate at St Luke's, Pallion, 1957-61.

The Reverend Canon Gordon Hopkins has been Vicar of St Luke's, Pallion, Sunderland, since 1939.

The Reverend Michael Keeling is Vicar of Acaster Selby with Appleton Roebuck, York, and author of *Morals in a Free Society*. He was Assistant Curate of St Luke's, Pallion, 1959-64.

The Reverend Father Barnabas Lindars is a member of the Society of St Francis and a Lecturer in Divinity in the University of Cambridge. He is author of *New Testament Apologetic*. He was Assistant Curate of St Luke's, Pallion, 1948-52.

PREFACE

The Church in England today is in some ways a church without walls. The position of privilege, derived from the Establishment, has largely disappeared before the tide of secularism, so that the Church of England cannot expect to have more favourable opportunities than are accorded to other Christian bodies, and indeed to other religious faiths. This is probably all to the good, in so far as it forces us to ecumenical thinking and to the recovery of the shattered unity of Christendom. More seriously, the defences of faith are in some measure crumbling, as widespread uncertainty about the fundamentals of Christian belief has invaded the minds even of those who are committed to Christianity and care deeply for the redemption of mankind. The task is just as meaningful and just as essential as it ever was, but the gospel message cannot be applied with the easy assurance that once seemed possible. There has been a welcome growth in compassion for man in his suffering, self-hatred, and self-destructiveness, but there is much less certainty about the answers. There is gain as well as loss here, and perhaps it is well that the walls of the Church should not be too high or too strong.

The changes that are going on all around us inevitably demand new patterns of ministry, so that the neat division of this country into parishes, each a community around the parish church, begins to look like a thing of the past. It would, however, be a gross oversimplification to suggest that the parish system has had its day. The parish will probably remain the basic unit of pastoral ministry in England for many years to come. But it will have to become much more flexible, so as to co-operate effectively with the pastoral groupings which cut across its boundaries, in education, industry, and community social service. Here again the

Church has to be without walls, ready to break out of traditional patterns and conventional habits of mind.

The essays in this book are all concerned with these problems from various points of view. The writers are united in the conviction that the parish church has a vital part to play in this time of spiritual and cultural revolution. But this can only be done if clergy and people alike are aware of what is going on around them. It would be a fatal mistake to try to build up the walls and to retreat behind them. There is no hard and fast line between the sacred and the secular, between believer and unbeliever, between the saved and the lost. There is a fluid interaction between them, demanding a wise and generous understanding, a flexible and delicate touch, on the part of all those who seek to make the Kingdom of God a living reality in our society today.

In "Worshippers Occasional and Lapsed", Colin Hickling begins the series by taking a closer look at the definition of "the congregation". Some of the implications of this are brought out in Ronald Bowlby's discussion of the situation of the newly ordained man in his essay on "Pastors and Parishioners" and in Gordon Hopkins' article "The Parish Church and the Industrial Worker". The next two essays, "The Challenge to Authority" and "Professors, Priests, and People", are concerned with changes in our climate of thought which need to be taken into account in presenting the Christian faith today. This leads to consideration of various aspects of the work of imparting Christianity—in teaching from the pulpit ("The Perils of Biblical Preaching") in making use of the results of serious theological scholarship ("Reading the Bible Today"), and by other techniques ("An Approach to Teaching"). Finally these issues are brought into relation with the current debate on education in Gordon Hopkins' "Willingly to School".

The views expressed here are those of each writer, and no attempt has been made to make them conform to a party line. But what unites them is more important than any contradictions between them, and this is derived in the first instance from a common parochial experience. Four of us served our first curacies in the same northern parochial parish, St Luke's, Pallion, Sunderland, under the same vicar, Canon Gordon Hopkins, who is the other contributor to this volume. Though we have moved into other spheres of ministry, the experience of the formative years in this place remains fundamental to all of us, and influences our thinking as we try to grapple with present problems. Some fourteen years ago a history of the parish was published, entitled *Pallion 1874–1954: Church and People in a Shipyard Parish*.[1] It was too much of a local history to attract wide interest, but many of those who did read it recognized that it had an importance greater than appeared at first sight. For the story of this shipyard parish is a microcosm of the story of the Church as a whole during those eighty years, in its own smaller way comparable in significance to G. K. A. Bell's famous life of Randall Davidson. The walls of the church were built in 1874, but the parish began without walls in 1868. Now, as the parish celebrates the centenary of its founding, it is fitting to look forward, and to try to discern new directions for the future. And so this volume is dedicated to the people of Pallion with gratitude and affection.

BARNABAS LINDARS, s.s.f.

---

[1] Published by the Wearside Printing Company, Sunderland, 1954.

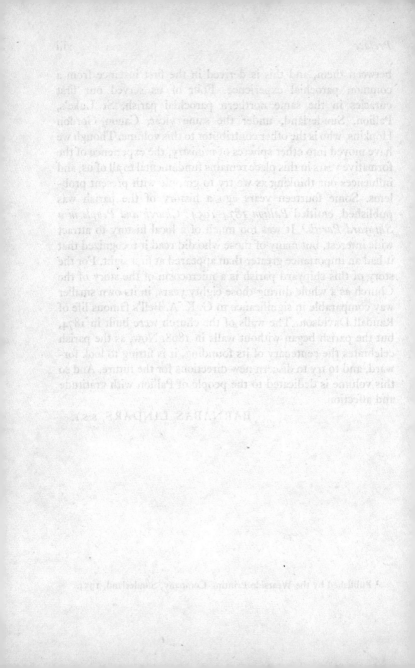

Worshippers Occasional and Lapsed
COLIN HICKLING

At one o'clock on Good Friday, for many years now, there has taken place at St Paul's church in the centre of Birmingham an event which deserves much meditation, especially when it is seen against the background of the contemporary practice of religion in England. There are a number of factories, large and small, in the neighbourhood, and from these between 700 and 1000 men and women of all ages and grades come to church for a short service. The vicar of St Paul's, Canon R. S. O. Stevens, the Industrial Missioner of the Diocese of Birmingham, describes the atmosphere at this service as being always most extraordinarily moving. On this occasion a group of working men and women are thus to be found in church, of whom not more than twenty per cent—so Canon Stevens estimates—have any kind of connection with the Church anywhere else.

How Religious is Britain?

Here, then, is an annual mass act of worship on the part of people whom others beside their own parish clergy, on the various estates around Birmingham, might well have written off as unchurched or "pagan". We may set it beside some other remarkable facts to which attention was drawn in David Martin's *Sociology of English Religion*. Drawing his evidence, it is true, from surveys based on the claims made by those questioned, rather than on the hard facts of church attendance figures, he makes the following remarkable statement:

> The important and massive fact remains that with every incentive to spend time in an alternative manner one quarter of the population is

in church at least once a month . . . In the course of a year nearly one
out of every two Britons will have entered a church, not for an event
in the life cycle or for a special personal or civic occasion, but for a
service within the ordinary pattern of institutional religion . . . Even
if one allows for some tendency to exaggerate attendance on the part
of those interrogated, that exaggeration is in itself significant.[1]

It is true that Martin also quotes the Church Information
Office figure of six per cent as the proportion of the population
who make their Easter communion in the Church of England.
This figure is almost identical with the proportion of respondents
in a National Opinion Poll survey who claimed to have attended
an Anglican place of worship "within the last seven days". No
doubt the comparison is a warning, if such were needed, that
people's own claims about their church attendance must be
taken cautiously. Nevertheless, even if Martin's conclusions seem
to be barely credible, his evidence at least suggests that large
sections of the English population do not *think of themselves* as
having "contracted out" of churchgoing to anything like the
extent assumed by a certain amount of thinking within the
church, especially by some kinds of pastoral theory and practice.

From the point of view of the sociologist of religion the practice
of attending church services is only one element in a wider assessment of the attitude of "the general run of people" towards
organized religion. Other criteria are at least as important in an
attempt to gauge the extent of "dechristianization" in this
country. These other criteria are indeed more nebulous in the
sense that it is difficult to provide solid evidence, or to interpret it
when gathered. Expressions of belief can be collected and collated:
people may be interrogated about, for example, a life beyond
death, or the Virgin Birth. But how should these data be assessed?
It is very doubtful whether in every case they represent a settled
conviction as opposed to a random offer of opinion on a matter

---

[1] David Martin, *Sociology of English Religion* (S.C.M. Press and Heine-
man, 1967), p. 5of.

which has been the subject of very little reflection. The replies may well indicate a failure of communication on the part of instructors in a recent or distant past, rather than the deliberate rejection of the Church's belief.

Equally ambiguous is such evidence of moral attitudes as is presented by Richard Hoggart in his book *The Uses of Literacy*.[1] To some extent, perhaps, he was describing a generation which was even then ceasing to be altogether typical. It was possible, when his book was written, to document a series of accepted moral attitudes, and to show that they were thought of as Christian: "After all, doing your best to be an 'ordinary decent person'—this is what Christianity means, really." The assumption that altruism *is* Christianity can hardly, indeed, be taken as evidence for an explicitly Christian attitude, since for centuries the Church has been the only teacher of morality. It had no rival during most of the period in the educational field, and there was no other body to do the job. These attitudes were accepted simply as correct, rather than as those appropriate to a church member. The enquirer who wishes to establish as objectively as he can the extent and nature of dechristianization feels he would like to hear further questions put to Hoggart's respondents. The answer might be illuminating.

In this connection we may quote the comment of a Trades Union member. He had been asked whether the reconciling and interpretative work he had come to value in the activity of a particular Industrial Mission would be as effectively done by any disinterested outside body, not necessarily Christian. It was interesting, though naturally no one can say how far it was a representative reaction, that he said it would not be the same. He did not make it clear why not. But his admission, made with some conviction although he was explicitly not a Christian believer (though a very occasional churchgoer!) at least indicates the com-

---

[1] Penguin Books, 1957, pp. 112f.

plexity of people's attitudes. This man fairly definitely identified the morality he had valued so highly with the Christian Church, even though his own personal disenchantment with the individual morality of churchgoers known to him had led to his deliberate rejection of church membership.

Few generalizations can be advanced with any safety. Neither the claim that "we are still basically an intensely religious and Christian people", nor the assertion that the "retreat from Christianity" has already involved an observable abandonment of positions once held, can be easily proved. For, as has been demonstrated in such a work as Wickham's *Church and People in an Industrial City*, the working masses have never to any great extent gone either to church or chapel. And yet the evidence just mentioned suggests widespread attitudes of approval both towards Christianity as such and towards the institutional Church.

Probably every part of the relevant evidence would vary enormously from one area to another. In the industrial North, for instance, positive attitudes towards the Church survive, together with other attitudes characteristic of an older generation of English working-class life, to a far greater extent than in the South-East. It may be true that miners still remember a Bishop of Durham who allowed his stables to be used as a prison for arrested strikers. It is also true that, in many areas of the North-East, the parish priest or the curate is asked indoors when he visits. He is treated as a man whose role in society is understood (largely, perhaps, in terms of the training of the young). In some areas of working-class London, by contrast, this is not the case. Even so, it is interesting that in post-war East London, where average church attendance is now for the most part extremely low, the purpose of a priest's visit may still be understood and his arrival welcomed. Clearly, a rich complexity of historical factors affects the issue. The collective memory is long, for good as well as for ill. In areas like Sunderland in the North and the

East End of London in the South, where faithful and penetrating pastoral work, and some relief work, were undertaken by some of the parish churches earlier in this century, the indications of respect for, and understanding of, the Church are still to be detected.

The assessment to be made by the sociologist is, then, one which must vary from region to region. Perhaps the still young science of religious sociology in this country will follow the example of the French and Italians in providing detailed evidence about areas other than the few which have already been made the subject of technical investigations. Their findings will still need interpretation. But one may guess that they will in many cases corroborate Martin's findings. There almost certainly exists, in large areas of the population, a considerable degree of adherence to Christianity understood as a system of ethics, and even some degree of assent to the concept of organized religion, even if this is seldom translated into practice.

Can you be a Christian without Going to Church?

All this may come to give rather more precise content to the aphorism that the Church of England is the Church "from which the people stay away". In other words, in a great number of cases it may still be plausibly urged that a man's own assessment of his standing *vis-à-vis* the Christian Church is not necessarily belied by the fact that, in practice, he is very seldom to be found inside a church. "Daddy, why don't you come to church?" "Who says I don't go to church?" father replies, and makes one of his six-monthly appearances. (This example is not imaginary.) This sort of pattern may still be not infrequent. The Northerner who says "We've always gone to St Luke's", though the last time anyone from the family darkened the doors was five years ago, should not perhaps be as quickly written off as a member of the Church as is sometimes the case. There probably still exists a much greater amount of goodwill towards the Church than is suggested by language about the "dear and lovable pagans" who, for example, want a church wedding for motives in which there may be "something very horrible".[1] And it is not enough to speak of goodwill. That in any case is the term used by the clergy, looking as it were over the walls surrounding their gathered congregation of faithful churchgoers. In a wide variety of degrees of articulate commitment, many of these "wellwishers" think of themselves not only as Christian but as members of the Church. It is a claim which requires more sensitive and thoughtful, and particularly more kind, reflection, than it often receives.

Thus the story is told of some members of a Church Youth Club who refused to make any further use of a certain garage to service their motor bikes on learning that the proprietor occasionally went to church. They themselves were "regular attenders", and had no doubt been instructed that weekly attendance at the Eucharist was the minimum required of a practising Christian. For them as perhaps for their parish priest, occasional conformity was simply a form of hypocrisy. But the garage proprietor himself might have been able in all sincerity, to present a different view of the case. His absences from weekly worship may have been due to a variety of reasons, rather than excuses, and it is highly improbable that in any sense—at least consciously—he had stayed away because he didn't really believe. "I'm afraid I've been rather busy" might be his reply to the Vicar if he had called, and it would probably have been a perfectly genuine statement. Had his attitude to churchgoing been both more perceptive and more convinced, no doubt his sense of priorities would have enabled him, somehow, to make his communion in spite of his preoccupations. But it was not necessarily his fault that his perceptiveness and conviction were imperfect.

How far has Dechristianization gone?

Two assumptions underlying a good deal of preaching and

[1] Martin Thornton, *Essays in Pastoral Reconstruction*, S.P.C.K. 1960, pp. 62, 75.

pastoral policy need, then, to be looked at more closely. First, "We live, as everyone knows, in a world that is largely post-Christian". So the preacher proclaims. And it is true and obvious that a wide range of pressures exist which act against Christian standards. The exploitation of sexual motifs in advertising is the most striking of these, though by no means the only example. Incitement to commit most of the deadly sins fills many pages of the advertising draughtsman's notebook. Moreover, advertising and the mass media are neither the only, nor the gravest, points at which pressure is exerted against Christian standards. The world into which the school-leaver is initiated on his or her first day of work, whether in an office or on the shop floor, is a different world from that of a churchgoing home and the Youth Fellowship. Many assumptions about human personality and values hold good there which harshly contradict what the adolescent concerned would have learned in confirmation classes. A "post-Christian world"; a world of "godless materialism"; there is obvious truth in the assumption.

Yet it is not the whole of the truth. The pressures are exerted by the mass media, but it does not necessarily follow that they are blindly complied with. Once again, the sociologist sees a more complex picture. The findings of his research may "bear strongly on assumptions about secularization, the impact of the age of science, the advent of human maturity, and so on. They suggest that far from being secular our culture wobbles between a partially absorbed Christianity, biased towards comfort and the need for confidence, and beliefs in fate, luck, and moral governance incongruously joined together." And even if "we add to these layers of folk religiosity the attraction of Freudianism and of Marxist mechanics for segments of the intelligentsia, it is clear that whatever the difficulties of institutional religion they have little connection with any atrophy of the capacity for belief."[1]

[1] David Martin, op. cit. p. 76.

The Problem of Defining Membership

The second assumption underlying much pastoral thought is to be distinguished from this last matter, though it is not unrelated and something has now already been said about it. The Easter-only communicant, the non-communicant Anglican who turns up at Mattins once in six weeks or so, the Sunday school parent (say) who in fact never goes to church at all—and for good measure we might add the family who go to church during a fortnight at Butlin's camp but at no other time, and the many for whom a Christmas carol service or a Remembrance Sunday parade are their annual act of worship, or even those who go to church once a year for the Good Friday service in St Paul's, Birmingham—it is assumed that all these are to be lumped together as "pagans" or "outsiders"; that they are to be regarded not only as being "on the fringe" (as indeed they are) or as being "sub-Christian" (in Martin Thornton's carefully defined but nevertheless rather patronizing word)[1] but also as being "no use to the Church". And the practical consequence is likely to be that they are at best marginal in the parish priest's approach to the organization of his week's work.

Once again, this assumption reflects *some* of the salient facts. The degree of commitment implied by the sort of religious practice just sketched contrasts sharply with the New Testament account of the church as outlined, for example, by Professor Paul Minear: "a called community whose origin and boundaries and destiny were determined by the powerful promises of him who sees the end from the beginning . . . a community in which the divine life, glory, and name were mediated afresh".[2] No one could doubt that, in many central ways at any rate, the weekly

[1] Martin Thornton, *Pastoral Theology: A Reorientation*, S.P.C.K. 1961, p. 166.
[2] Paul Minear, *Images of the Church in the New Testament*, Lutterworth, 1961, p. 224.

communicant participating enthusiastically in stewardship and contributing to regular discussion groups—the keen layman as much modern pastoralia sees him—is reproducing much of the New Testament pattern of Christianity, whereas the laxer "occasional conformists" fail to do so. To this extent the original protest of English nonconformity, which is still implied in their ideal of the gathered Church, is a correct one.

But this "rigorist" assumption—for want of a more inclusive term—is right, like so much else, in what it affirms, but is to be questioned in what it denies. The occupant of the "fringe" of Anglican practice remains, after all, a baptized person; and remains also (where no explicit option in a different direction has been made) a participant in a culture in which the Christian "staining" (to use the Bishop of Middleton's metaphor)[1] has been long-standing, wide, and penetrating. The pressures acting against regular church attendance are manifold, and the sensitive pastor will surely be sympathetic towards their effect. It is easier for the older and more leisured members of his congregation to resist them than it is for the vast majority of those to whom (according to the ideals of the Ordinal) he is appointed to minister. The pressures of time and of fatigue are often considerable.

So too, it is worth adding, are some social pressures of a kind not always very carefully thought of. There are areas of professional life, to take a ridiculous example which nevertheless operates in some cases, in which golf plays a role which is more than one of physical and mental recreation. And golf is played on Sundays. If indeed—in other professional walks of life in this country, as in greater measure in the United States—church-going too may be socially and professionally profitable, neither

[1] E. R. Wickham, *Church and People in an Industrial City*, Lutterworth 1957, p. 230. Wickham uses the metaphor in a different context: he is describing what he urges as the right *future* influence of the church on society: "the situation where the Church . . . seeks neither to manipulate nor dominate the world, nor to escape from it, nor merely to reflect a voluntarist religious aspect of it, but to understand it, prophesy within it, interpret it, and stain it."

case justifies an unreservedly hard judgement. However deplorable, a professional rat race exists.

The Embarrassments of being "Religious"

What is more to the point, and harder to weigh up, is the reluctance of most people to become identifiable as "religious". "If one of their number", says Hoggart, "is strikingly affected by the dogmas of religion, they are quick to say, 'Oh, 'e's got religious mania'."[1] A non-Roman Catholic adult's attendance at Church services, if it is as frequent as once a week, is in many social strata liable to criticism almost equally damaging. The answer of the "rigorist" at this point is quick but unfair. Unfailingly regular presence at the Eucharist is part of a Christian's witness. If it evokes criticism, this is a kind of minor persecution which must be accepted as part of the cost of being a Christian. Translated into the language of the people, this comes out rather differently. You can't be a Christian at all, it seems, without "being very religious".

There is a real and powerful pressure which is to a great extent responsible for the lapse of the young and for the abstentions of those making their careers. It is a pressure which asks for much patience and understanding. We cannot, after all, alter history. The Church of England abrogated at the Reformation its basis in Canon Law for making weekly Sunday churchgoing formally *de rigueur*. For a time, indeed, a statutory obligation replaced the canonical one. But this was an exercise of compulsion which we now find embarrassing. The results of this are inescapable. No statement of the duty of Sunday churchgoing exists at any more formally authoritative level than the short list of recommendations by the two Archbishops. We are dealing with a situation in which weekly churchgoing—and even more weekly communion —are regarded by the majority essentially as devout practices. For most people, in any case, no convincing reason has ever been

[1] Richard Hoggart, op. cit. p. 116.

shown why churchgoing should be an indispensable part of what it means to be a Christian. The contrast with the Roman Catholic situation is sharp but clear. The point may be illustrated by a rather extreme example. A highly intelligent shop steward in a ship-building concern narrated to a small discussion group his "conversion" (it was his own word) from an ethic of sectional self-interest to "Christianity" (again, his own word). He made only one appearance in church over quite a lengthy period at the time concerned. And he seemed totally unaware of any incongruity in this. On the basis of what he had gathered to be the true nature of Christianity, there was no reason why he should regard his absence from church as incongruous. He was not, he might have said, a "very religious man". If he had been, no doubt he would have "gone to church more often". If we are to accept a person of this sort as he is—and he is the kind of character it is most vital for the Church to see sharing in her ministry to the world—then we must accept, provisionally at least, his own assessment of the situation. We may not judge him by standards he has never seen reason to accept. We must note, and for the time being respect, his distinction between "being religious" and "being Christian". This reluctance to be identified as "being religious" must be recognized as a real and understandable pressure counting formidably against standards which all would wish, ideally, to see put into practice.

A Weakening of Confidence

One further pressure to which lay people are exposed needs to be thought of; one which is clearly not unrelated to the last question. Lord Eccles probably speaks for many when he describes his disenchantment with the Churches coupled with a continuing fascination by the New Testament. "The nearer to the gospels, the further from religion . . . I felt less and less sympathy with Christianity as expounded by the churches."[1] This compares

[1] Lord Eccles, *Halfway to Faith*, Geoffrey Bles, 1966, p. 66.

closely with the popular jibe at the hypocrisy of churchgoers. But, in addition, more intellectual dissuasives play their part. The notion of a *trahison des clercs* is perhaps more influential still than we realize. Very large numbers of people visited the Dead Sea Scrolls exhibition recently displayed in the British Museum, and heard Dr Allegro and others commenting on their significance. Some at least among them will have been looking for confirmation of their suspicion that institutional Christianity is an invention of the Church. Awareness that such suspicions—and more than suspicions—have been widely held may well be among the pressures tending to diminish confidence in the "professional Christians". We must also take into account the influence of sceptical attitudes of this kind among those responsible for the teaching of religion in many schools. Some of this may help to explain a certain ambivalence in many people's attitude to the clergy. If they like the Vicar their approval may be warm and bring with it a real affection for the parish church. But if he is not personally acceptable the criticism of both may be equally bitter. But in either case the remoteness of the Church as institution, and of the religious services it conducts, may have been increased by the factors outlined.

Need for Pastoral Imagination

These, then, are some of the forces which in the contemporary scene render churchgoing a hard option for the ordinary citizen. It is true that in a minority of cases this may be an attraction. An Oxford undergraduate admitted to the writer that it was more fun being a practising Christian when one knew it was a minority activity. For most that would hardly be the case. Once "church-leaving age" has been reached (to use a happy expression coined by the parent of a Sunderland boy who had lapsed from his Communion), then the tragic lapse will occur in the majority of cases. The adolescent moves into the pattern of normal adult life, in whatever social stratum it may be. And he realizes that there is no compelling reason (none at any rate of which he has been deeply convinced) [why he should go to church more than very infrequently, and he senses many reasons why he should not.

But the wise and pastorally-minded priest will surely not write off such a young man, or his girl friend, or indeed their parents, as simply "lapsed". He will not assume that there is no longer any point in visiting the home; that these are simply two more faces that have become submerged again in the mire of the "materialistic world". Rather, he will attempt to remain in touch in so far as time allows. He will continue to greet these people as friends (and this is after all a more real basis for the pastoral relationship than any other). In due course, he will be able to set about their preparation for marriage as one who is, in a remoter but still real way, their pastor and guide.

What has been said may be summed up in the words of a recent German writer, Joachim Matthes. "Is not this 'remote adherence' ['distanzierte Kirchlichkeit'], under specific social conditions, a form of adherence which corresponds entirely to the facts, and which therefore gives us no right to speak (in the type of case under discussion, that is) of dechristianization ['Entkirchlichung']?"[1] Dr Vidler makes a similar claim in reminding us that "the Church of England is accustomed to providing a home, albeit often a distant one, for all sorts and conditions of men", and repeats an earlier writer's assertion that "the distinctive mission of the Church of England is the Apostolate of the Indevout".[2]

Now the "home", clearly, cannot be one in which all is understood and therefore all is permitted. The apostolate is a real work of education directed towards Christian maturity, in which

---

[1] *Die Emigration der Kirche aus der Gesellschaft* ("The Church's Emigration from Society"), Furche-Verlag, 1964, p. 40.

[2] "Religion and the National Church" in *Soundings*, Cambridge, 1962, p. 260.

every part of a responsible man or woman's life is to be consecrated through their participation in Christ's redemption. This
participation implies the Eucharist, and ideally—this is surely
beyond serious question—the weekly Sunday Eucharist. But
people must be approached where they are, with proper pastoral
affection and respect. And they must be led on from there at
whatever pace, and to whatever next step, may be appropriate
for them. Martin Thornton, for whom the devout "remnant"
seems at times all-important, is careful to outline an educative
pastoral care of those whom he would call the "sub-Christians".[1]
Every sensitive and alert priest will certainly look for opportunities to exercise this pastoral care in appropriate ways where-
ever he can. And he will probably feel a greater respect than
Thornton implies for the real ethical achievements of the Spirit
in many of those whose adherence is, in the German terminology,
"at a distance".

Value of Industrial Mission

What could this involve in practice? Two examples may be given.
First, the following change of role was urged at a discussion
between a small group of men in different levels of industrial
concerns and a group of junior clergy in the London Diocese. One
of the men from industry said that he thought all the clergy ought
to be doing the work now undertaken by industrial chaplains. It
was a wild exaggeration. And yet there is a valuable pointer here
for those able to re-order their priorities in such a way as to set
more time at their own disposal. It is sometimes possible, for
example, for the parish priest to visit an industrial concern with
which his parish has some contact. It goes without saying that
the greatest possible courtesy and responsibility is needed in any
such approach. Great harm could be done, and a most unfortunate impression given, if the vicar went round the shop floor
without the full consent of the Trades Union representatives

[1] *Pastoral Theology : A Reorientation*, pp. 168f.

concerned. Indeed, at the meeting just mentioned, the fear was expressed that some of the functions of the latter might have been usurped by the chaplain. But the value of such visiting may be considerable; not least, in 'one instance known to the writer, since this gave precisely the opportunity to remain in friendly informal contact with the "lapsed" of which mention was made earlier.

This corresponds closely with the experience of the country priest meeting his people in the street, at the shop, and at the end of his garden. It is a "friendly contact" largely absent from town life, and of immense value. But it would be altogether wrong to see the presence of the priest in the factory as in any kind of way another technique of "fishing". "Fishing" is indeed a metaphor with the highest possible authority,[1] and no one would deny that to recruit, where he can, is a part of the priest's work. Indeed, it is an essential part of the work of the whole Church. But the presence of a member of the clergy as an accepted and even welcomed guest in an industrial concern is for other purposes than that. What these other purposes may involve can be illustrated by the comment of a works manager in a small engineering works. It was, he said, through conversation with a curate from the parish church (who visited regularly in this factory) that he had first been enabled to see his job as a Christian activity governed by Christian principles. The fact that the man concerned is himself a very occasional communicant, yet a person of great Christian integrity in his approach to his work, itself underlines some of the points made earlier.

Secondly, it is appropriate to mention a small discussion group initiated in the parish for whose centenary this book is written. The group was first formed during a Lent project conducted by a Franciscan Friar. As it has developed over the years, it has become an occasion when men with a wide variety of industrial experience and of degrees of church-attachment have met

[1] Mark 1.17.

regularly to discuss issues of concern to them. Talks have been given, for example, by a leading Trade Unionist and by a member of the Economics faculty at the University of Durham. The meetings take place in the Vicar's sitting-room. From time to time explicitly theological issues emerge. The present writer remembers, for example, an impressively unassuming account by a Roman Catholic of the way in which he had come to regard his work as the offering which he contributed towards that day's Mass. The thought is a commonplace of ascetic theology, but was impressive as contributed on an occasion such as the one described. An activity like this, lying mid-way between the pastoral concern of the parish Church and the enterprise of adult education, is surely one for which there are many fruitful openings.

Other examples might be given of the working out of an approach which "takes people where they are" and accepts some kind of adherence in distance to the life and prayer of the parish church. It seems a pity, for instance, to be cynical about the occasional offices, at which the clergy have been said to function as little more than druids, or about services, like those on Mothering Sunday, which sometimes draw considerable numbers. All these occasions afford a hearing for imaginative and responsible correction of people's misconceptions, and for a thoughtful presentation of Christian faith calculated to speak, and to be heard in, "their language". More important, it may be possible to articulate what is half-Christian in the attitudes of those involved so as to evoke a fuller response. On rare occasions, too, an individual of outstanding pastoral gifts is able to draw considerable numbers of the relatively unchurched to an act of worship. This too constitutes an opportunity both to persuade individuals and to affect the local climate of opinion.

The consequences of the policy sketched out for pastoralia might be further illustrated. The parish magazine may include in a "personal column" information about personalities connected in various ways with the church or the local community even though everyone knows they have not been to church for years. There may be an article discussing a crisis in local industry. The obituary of prominent local figures may acknowledge fully and gratefully the contribution they have made to the life of the area. More urgently, there should be a good deal of "worldliness" of the kind here roughly indicated in the teaching of the young. The training of adolescents, before *and after* confirmation, centres to a great extent around the nature of Christian responsibility. On any good theological basis, therefore, it must surely include the discussion of a variety of matters of, at first sight, exclusively secular interest in the fields of politics and industrial practice.

Church Without Walls

Horst Symanowski writes this about the "congregation without walls". "At which points can we still erect a wall *in* the congregation, *around* the congregation, or *outside* the congregation? The answer is, Nowhere, for if we do that, we cease to be a congregation."[1] There is a criticism here which applies to much in present Anglican pastoral policy. "The Lord's people around the Lord's table on the Lord's day", and "The Christian family gathered for the family's worship", are slogans which well affirm the solidarity of the congregation at prayer and the unity which the eucharist effects. They proclaim vital truths about the Church, as Ronald Bowlby points out. But both slogans, like all slogans, are over-simplified. Both may be misunderstood in terms of a congregationalism which loses sight of the whole Church in time and space (the real unity sacramentally expressed at the altar). And they also turn attention away from the large and important penumbra of men and women who are "adherents at distance". They ought, of course, to be around the Lord's table. But their absence may not be wholly their own fault. "Invincible

[1] *The Christian Witness in an Industrial Society*, Collins, 1966, p. 108.

ignorance" will have played its part in some cases. And they may often have a distinctively Christian commitment at a moral level. Their membership of the Church is more than potential, even though it seems so seldom to get to the point of concrete expression in the terms we should want.

We must not build walls which would leave these people outside. We must not allow them to suspect that the Vicar is "only interested in those who go". The Church needs the co-operation of its less committed members if the next generation is not to see a "dechristianization" of a much more palpable kind. To put it more positively (and more in line with the points developed by Symanowski) the Church's ministry to those furthest from the fire may well be better helped by those who, as it were, stand half-way than by those nearest to the fire. Let us hope then for some kind of pastoral practice—if men can be found with the stamina to carry it out—which will balance the "intensive" work of building up the eucharistic congregation of "regulars" with a genuine and patient ministry to the "distant adherents", and above all a ministry built on respect for them and on trust and hope in the Christ who is in them.

Pastors and Parishioners

RONALD BOWLBY

What does it feel like to start work in a parish? Reactions differ, but it is commonplace to find a marked loss of confidence and the sense of direction blurred or destroyed.

The schoolteacher fresh from college will probably be given thirty or more periods a week as soon as he arrives. The managerial recruit may spend some months learning the work of a department, but he will be alongside people who are clear about their place and function in the supervisory chain.

By contrast the Anglican curate faces a pattern of life in which the parts seem at first unconnected. There is a curious and worrying feeling of not being "involved". While there are certain specific things to be "done" (such as taking a Sunday service or preaching), far more time is set aside for vague and prolonged activities like "study" and "visiting". The new deacon has been used to studying for exams, but to what end is it now required? And how does one set about it largely unsupervised and alone? Visiting is difficult because it is not at first related to any specific need, and sheer strangeness creates barriers which seem frighteningly high.

Early in his ministry he will probably be allocated responsibility for some of the parochial organizations. These will vary from those concerned with teaching children (like the Sunday school) to those whose emphasis is more social and diffused. Here are jobs to be done; but here also are the *bêtes noires* of most theological colleges for the past fifteen years, since they seem to symbolize the anxiety of the church to cling to its institutional life. Hence the work is accepted with mixed feelings about its use in the Church today.

3

Again, while most vicars hold a weekly "staff meeting", this is often severely practical in its range: *ad hoc* decisions about who will do what during the coming week, with the occasional discussion of this or that problem as it rears its head. There may be an underlying pastoral strategy, but it does not often "come through", except in terms of keeping everything going as well as possible. And while this is not an undesirable aim for the particular, it fails to unite the various particulars within any cohesive, purposive pattern or whole.

The new curate remains bewildered. Friendship in the parish and familiarity with certain kinds of work ease the tension, it is true. But he remains aware that today there are many other agencies working alongside him in the field of human welfare, a fact in which his vicar may sometimes seem rather uninterested. The highly personal, one-by-one ideal of pastoral ministry, as it is delineated in the Ordinal, hardly seems to fit the demands of a modern urban parish. The emergence of a secular society has not destroyed the enormous fund of goodwill which still exists for some Christian values and for most clergy as individuals; but it has created a critical attitude towards the Church as an institution, which has made the work of a priest vastly more difficult. It has always been physically demanding, as a man fresh from college soon finds! But now it is also emotionally and intellectually demanding, because ways of worship, faith, and much else are continually called in question.

With such varied pressures upon him, it is clear that the newcomer's transition from ordinand to deacon and priest is rarely a painless one. But after many years of academic studies it is often a great relief to start doing something and being paid for it, even if the bewilderment remains. What cannot be denied, I think, is that the balance easily swings too far the other way. Study is soon dropped altogether; bewilderment is overlaid by a kind of "busyness" which lasts until middle age, and then evaporates into routine. Others, aware of the painful loss of integrity which such an attitude can involve, look around for other means of expressing their vocation which are not so closely tied to the parochial ministry.

The Need for a Theology of Mission

The root of the trouble may often lie in a lack of theology; that is, a lack of thought about what God is doing in his world, and about his purpose for it. My own conviction is that pastoral work becomes frustrating when it is dissociated from the Church's mission. It is fundamentally important for every priest to ask—and keep on asking—"What is the contemporary Church for?"

Once that question is faced, theological thinking can begin. One is forced back to the scriptures, to an understanding of contemporary society, ethics, liturgy, and so on. Of course there are other questions to be asked, in a world which finds it increasingly difficult to accept the idea of God at all. But in the context of the priest's work, the question of the Church's mission is central, since it is the answer to this question which can unify work and policy, and which prevents one's ministry collapsing into a series of unrelated compartments.

It may help to indicate the scope of what is meant if we look more closely at the New Testament doctrine of the Church as the Body of Christ. It is significant that the particular doctrine finds expression in part as a result of the pastoral problems which arose in the new congregation at Corinth. St Paul finds there jealousy, lack of care and disorder in worship (1 Cor. 11.17–22). He uses the analogy of a human body to explain that the Church has a variety of different organs which are interdependent in the same way. "For just as the body is one and has many members, and all the members of the body, though many, are one body, so it is with Christ." (1 Cor. 12.12, RSV.)

Different members of the Church have different gifts which will enable the whole Church to function effectively. The

purpose of this is elaborated in a magnificent passage from the
Epistle to the Ephesians (4.1–16), a veritable manifesto. Here we
find the qualities which are to mark the lives of *all* Christians—
"lowliness, meekness, patience", and especially eagerness "to
maintain the unity of the Spirit in the bond of peace". But within the "one body" there is differentiation "according to the
measure of Christ's gift". And so the various ministries within
the Church are listed—apostles, prophets, evangelists, pastors,
and teachers. But this does not mean any fragmentation in the
life of the Church, for all serve a common end. Each one has his
part to play in the complex process of "building up the body of
Christ". This means far more than creating a lively congregation,
conscious of itself as "the Church". It is a formative work at a
deeper level, aiming to bring people "to the unity of the faith and
of the knowledge of the Son of God, to mature manhood, to the
measure of the stature of the fulness of Christ". In so far as this
is achieved, Christ, who is the head of the body, is the principle
of life in all the members. Built up into him, they draw their life
from him. So "we are to grow up in every way into him who is
the head, into Christ, from whom the whole body, joined and
knit together by every joint with which it is supplied, when each
part is working properly, makes bodily growth and upbuilds
itself in love".

Christ, who is the head of the Church (Col. 1.18) continues his
work and mission through the Church. And in this sense it is true
to say that mission is the first task of the Church, a theological
understanding which might draw especially on such passages as St
John 17, or the well known verse of St Matthew: "Go therefore
and make disciples of all the nations, baptizing them in the name
of the Father and of the Son and of the Holy Spirit, teaching
them to observe all that I commanded you; and lo, I am with you
always, to the close of the age" (Matt. 28.19f).

Professor J. G. Davies, in his recent book *Worship and Mission*[1]

[1] S.C.M. Press, 1966, pp. 31f.

has warned against the danger of too close an association of mission with the doctrine of the Church:

> The recovery of the doctrine of the Church as the Body of Christ has been one of the most significant theological advances of the present century; it is not surprising therefore that the modern investigation into the meaning of mission should have become associated with ecclesiology, but this is not a direct association that should be endorsed . . . Nevertheless just as, for example, the doctrine of the Church cannot be isolated from Christology or Pneumatology, so mission and Church have a relation, although the starting point for investigating it is not ecclesiology but the being and purpose of God.

Failure to recognize the primacy of mission may be one reason why pastoral confusion enters in. Certainly one must then go on to discuss what kind of mission, and here again the emphasis of biblical and other thinking has shifted considerably in recent years. It is no longer enough to think of mission as the attempt to draw people into an institution from "outside". Canon Douglas Webster has put this finely:

> Although we cannot fathom the mystery of mission we can perceive some of its patterns. In Holy Scripture and in the history and experience of the Church it is clear that mission is no simple, one-way, one-level movement. It is composed of two movements in four directions. There is the perpendicular movement of the Gospel, redeeming love coming down to earth and lifting up the redeemed people of God to his own heights. And there is the horizontal rhythmic movement of the church in its relation with the world, going out as diaspora, dispersed for witness and loving service, and returning inward and together as ecclesia for fellowship and worship. When this horizontal movement of out and in is continually intersected by that other movement of the eternal Gospel which is up and down, mission is taking place. The results we do not know and cannot judge. But the ultimate pattern is a cross.[1]

[1] *Unchanging Mission*, Hodder and Stoughton, 1965, p. 79.

The Pastoral Implications of Mission

The mission of the people of God is to declare his love in a secular world by the quality of their service and life together in the body of Christ. What are the pastoral implications of this theological "starting point"?

First, the parochial congregation (for it is that about which this essay is mainly concerned) is an interdependent unity and fellowship. The task of the priest is not least to draw out an understanding of this truth within the life of the Church, so that the Body of Christ grows to a more mature "stature" or effectiveness in its work. In recent years there have been many books on the role and place of the laity in the Church. More work perhaps needs to be done on the priesthood of the whole Church, and the nature of the ordained priesthood within it. But there has been a welcome recognition of the active nature of the lay vocation, and of the demands which this makes on priest and people alike. Older books on pastoralia tended to stress the idea of the priest as the shepherd who was constantly caring for the "flock". Admittedly this is one of the biblical images. But sheep strike most of us as passive and nervous animals, hardly likely to contribute to a useful discussion on the best way of running the farm! In practical terms there has been a tradition of diligent house-to-house visiting by the parish priest or his curate, which has had the undoubted and necessary benefit of enabling the priest to know his people. It fails very easily to produce within the congregation knowledge of one another. The insights of contemporary society also point to the importance of the small group. A pastoral strategy might suggest that individual visiting by the pastor is likely to be more valuable and more purposeful if it is seen as one means of drawing the congregation together in mutual support, rather than creating widespread dependence on the ordained ministry.

Second, the work of teaching and training becomes more

integrated with world as well as Church, when we see the priest's work as that of helping men and women to interpret and express their mission in society with sensitive discernment and effectiveness. St Luke's, Pallion, was one of the few parishes where a sustained and determined attempt was made to equip young apprentices and others with a Christian understanding of their work and the society in which they were growing up. The Christian Workers Union in that parish[1] used small groups, which seemed an essential ingredient in the success of this approach—an experience confirmed by similar work among adults at Billingham, in industrial missions, and elsewhere. It remains true, sadly, that the new curate may well find himself in a parish where no continuous teaching of this kind will go on except with children. The assumption that Confirmation represents the end-point of education in the Body of Christ (apart from sermons, I suppose) hangs heavily over much Anglican pastoral work. It is time for its burial.

Third, there are enormous consequences from this for our understanding of liturgy and its place in the Church's life. It is interesting that it was quite possible to go through different theological colleges in the fifties and early sixties without having heard of Hebert's *Liturgy and Society*,[2] for instance, and without being aware that liturgy was anything more than a study of different rites.[3] In reality, the people who form the Body of Christ are most likely to absorb a deeper understanding of their vocation through "doing the Eucharist" week by week. Much depends on the way it is done (though perhaps not quite so much as devoted advocates of this or that "position" sometimes imagine!). In the Eucharist the world is not left out. Here we participate in Christ, and so renew our share in his mission. In

[1] See *Note* on p. 30.
[2] Faber and Faber, 1935.
[3] Cf. the remarks in J. A. T. Robinson, *On Being the Church in the World*, S.C.M. Press, p. 63.

the Eucharist the truth of our dependence upon God and one
another is reaffirmed in the Word, and acted out by the shared
confession and communion. Here men may see material things
offered and consecrated, as a reminder of what Bishop Westcott
called "the destiny of the whole". Here especially men may
submit to the demands of perfect love, and offer their life in
union with the sacrifice of Christ their Head.

No longer does it become a question of "taking a service", or
of preaching a sermon in the manner of a lecture. Liturgy must
be related to the life of the Church, and it is important that the
whole Church tries to work out what this means in practice for
their own congregational life. At a parish meeting, a lifelong
churchman (in his forties) suddenly asked why the vicar wanted
their opinion anyway: "It's your job to decide what sort of
services we have." Yet it was that same man who later remarked
that he and his family felt more involved in worship than they
had ever done before, and so it meant more to them. You cannot
stress the mission of the people of God in life if it is being denied
by their practice and understanding of worship.

Fourth, an emphasis on the relation of pastoral method to a
theology of the church raises questions about the care of individuals. It can be rather disappointing to the new curate when he
finds that people do not flock to him for help; the more so as he
looks enviously over his shoulder at the local G.P. or the R.C.
priest with his penitents. This is deceptive. There is an enormous
demand for help, but it does not show itself in religious forms at
first. In one way or another the new priest has to learn to listen
and accept, realizing that in many people's eyes he remains a
symbol of duty and censoriousness rather than of mercy and
encouragement. What matters in the end is the reality of the
priest's own commitment, and perhaps especially in prayer.
While this essay is primarily concerned with the interlocking of
theology and pastoralia, it should not be forgotten that these also
interlock most deeply and costingly in a man's prayer. Or they

should. Out of such prayer can come the compassion and strength which are still fundamental to the priest's ministry, together with the knowledge which can release this or that person from fears and sins, back into the service of God and the life of the Church.

This leads to a final point, which is that the priest's ministry is never to be seen as in competition with that of other workers in the secular field, nor in isolation from it.

> There will in fact be little progress towards a new establishment unless the clergy know and have learned to cooperate with health visitors, maternity and child welfare workers, hospital almoners, education welfare officers and teachers, children's officers, civic welfare and other old people's services, housing managers and their staffs, mental welfare officers, and the probation service. The list sounds, and is, formidable. But these are the new pastors of our people, and unless we know and are known as having an integral place in this array we must not be surprised if many of our parishioners think of us as marginal to society and its "real" needs.[1]

Pastoralia unrelated to a theology of mission and the Church will find such activities "threatening", instead of recognizing that our prime concern as pastors has always been to build up the Church for its work in the world, work which in certain aspects is rightly being done by social agencies of many kinds.

Bishop Simon Phipps makes a similar point in his recent book *God on Monday*.[2] He decries a theology which fails to see the need for partnership with those who already work in the neighbourhood as part of the pastoral concern of the modern welfare state. He suggests two contributions which the priest may be able to make; first, certain insights of Christian thinking, and second, "to be an integrating force, in a special way, among what might remain a series of separate individuals".

[1] Alfred Jowett, in *The English Church: a New Look*, ed. Leslie Hunter, 1965, pp. 101–2.
[2] Hodder and Stoughton, 1966, pp. 80–1.

Training for the Ordained Ministry

It is significant that the phrase "training for the ministry" is generally used in the sense "training before ministry begins". Yet our Lord's training of the Twelve took place within the context of an active ministry, and was followed by a tremendous growth of theological understanding and learning *after* the resurrection.

During my time at a theological college I went away for six months to do unskilled work in a machine shop in a large works in Coventry. This was administratively inconvenient, and it was good of the Principal to let me go. One immediate effect of this experience was to make me feel more dissatisfied with the institutional Church and to hesitate about entering the parochial ministry. Another effect—a more important one, perhaps—was to heighten my existing awareness that one cannot easily learn to think theologically about the world during two short academic years. The process can certainly *begin* there, more readily than is sometimes supposed; but one recognizes the great difficulty which colleges have in trying to balance the needs of academic training against the demand to be more "involved" with the secular life.

Once a deacon or priest, however, the difficulty should be much less. But often it isn't. This is sometimes attributed to the fact that the clergyman wears different clothes and spends more time in the church building. But a deeper cause may lie in the failure to provide an ongoing exchange between theological thinking and the pastoral and social realities which now press in.

The Church of England still expects most of its clergy to work on their own. It seems to be assumed that the clergyman must therefore think and read entirely on his own. A significant change of emphasis has taken place. The ordinand did plenty of personal reading as a student, but he subjected the fruits of his reading to the comments of a tutor, as well as discussing it in a seminar and talking informally with others on many occasions.

Even as a curate such exchange of ideas and experience is likely to become difficult, apart from the somewhat varied provision of a post-ordination training course. Later it may become more difficult still. St Luke's Vicarage, Pallion, was a clergy house, a rare (but not rarefied) situation. No one will ever know how often the hooks of theology were fitted to the eyes of experience within the steaming walls of the kitchen or the bathroom! But in so doing, pastoral work became meaningful and the burden was shared.

I believe that this process can best go forward through commitment to a group—and of course the group need not consist only of clergy. Since the pastoral worker is unlikely to meet the university scholar face to face, it is necessary to wrestle together with the biblical texts and the fruits of such scholarship, and to relate them to the actual work of building up the Body of Christ in their own place. The present trend towards group or team ministries is not as new as it looks,[1] and joint study should be one of its main benefits. But as yet one does not see much sign that such study has the place it should in such teams. We do not find it easy, because we have leaned so heavily on the professional teacher in the past. It is also demanding in time and preparation, since there is little value in coming to study the Bible together if no one has read the passage or consulted a commentary beforehand.

At another level, perhaps it is worth stressing the obvious point that those who study and teach full-time have their first commitment to the Church as a whole, and not just to its student part. One of the lecturers in a theological college was invited to join in some meetings associated with an industrial mission and new estate parish. He said subsequently that this experience had altered the whole emphasis of his teaching in the college.

[1] E.g. in the organization of the minster system in Anglo-Saxon England, though this was "only suited to a church in the missionary stage" (G. W. O. Addleshaw, *The Beginning of the Parochial System*, St Anthony's Hall Publications, 1953, p. 15). Are we now returning to that stage?

Again the bewilderment of the newly ordained man would perhaps be less, if he did not so often lose close contact with almost all senior clergy except his own vicar. Just as "parochial education" almost stops dead at Confirmation, so "ministerial education" almost stops dead at ordination. In these days it is not enough to leave the individual to read in isolation, and it runs contrary to most of what we know about normal processes of learning.

Since most contemporary ordinands have not had a university education, the last point possesses added force. Not all priests need to be scholars in the normal sense of the word; but all priests need to know how to relate the fruits of scholarship to their work, and it becomes particularly urgent that those who *are* scholars should study the demands on communication which this situation creates. The Church is beginning to show greater concern for "training its laity" and building up the Body of Christ. Parallel with this, I believe, must go an equal concern for "training its clergy", so that theology may issue in a missionary and pastoral strategy which is constructive and meaningful in the society to which we all belong.

NOTE

The Christian Workers Union aimed to train adolescents during their first years of work along the lines developed by the late Canon Cardijn in the Roman Catholic Jocist movement (Jeunesse Ouvrière Chrétienne, known in this country as Young Christian Workers). The boys and girls concerned met in small groups, and their meetings followed Cardijn's "enquiry method". This has been described, and the outline and results of thirteen "enquiries" given, in *The Parish Church and the Young Worker*, edited by C. H. G. Hopkins (S.P.C.K., 1963). The following quotations indicate the principles adopted: "The section selects its own chairman and secretary so that the clergy are at the meeting in an advisory capacity to give help as and when it is needed.

It is an essential part of the training that the meeting should as far as possible be conducted by the young workers themselves, even though at first some of them may be inarticulate . . . The enquiry system aims at enabling the young worker to arrive gradually and by implication for himself at a specifically Christian conviction in matters of belief and conduct. The section, through question and answer, is pooling information and ideas, and from these a general impression is being formed. To get beyond this, the group must be helped to form a clearer judgement and arrive without prejudice at a definite conviction" (p. 7).

The Parish Church and the Industrial Worker[1]

GORDON HOPKINS

The parish of Pallion is a mile and a half up-stream from the mouth of the river Wear. It is in the centre of an enormous concentration of industry, and from the Alexandra bridge there is a panoramic view of industrial life, which must be unequalled in extent and character: six shipyards, six engine works, two large collieries, the enormous Pyrex glass works, and the works of the largest cranebuilding corporation in the world. Beyond lies the large Pallion Trading Estate, with a variety of factories, the biggest of which include the Bristol Siddeley aero-engine works, and David Brown's engineering works, along with the Thorn A.E.I. Electrical Industries. Some of the factories on the Trading Estate, and especially the clothing factory, employ a very large number of girls and women.

Wartime Beginnings

In the early days of the war it was not difficult to make contact with the shipbuilding and marine engineering industries in the parish, especially since the Vicar's previous seven years had been in a shipbuilding parish on Merseyside. During a long number of years in Pallion, it had been possible, gradually, to get to know a very large number of people engaged in varying kinds of work in local industrial life. At no time has life for most of them been plain sailing or easy for very long, and people are glad of the chance to talk informally about a great many different facets of industrial life, with its problems and difficulties. Basically, of

[1] Reprinted, with the Editor's permission, from *Theology*, Vol 69, pp. 549–53 (December 1966), where it was the fifth in a symposium of six essays on *Industrial Mission*.

course, most of these problems are essentially human in nature and origin, and there is no difficulty whatever in describing the relationship that is gradually built up between the parish priest and the people he has met as being "pastoral" in character.

During the war, a great deal of work was set on foot in the parish amongst adolescent boys and girls. At that time nearly all the boys in the parish became apprentices in one of the shipyards or forges. The men in the works and the yards, along with the foremen and management, seemed to be quite genuinely interested in all this club work that was going on amongst these lads in industry. So here was a valuable additional point of contact.

In the early 1940s, the present Dean of Chester (G. W. O. Addleshaw), along with the present Bishop of Accra (Richard Roseveare, SSM), were deeply concerned to discover whether something similar to continental Jocism could be made to work amongst young industrial workers who were members of the Church in this country. Quite a considerable number of young workers were trained in Pallion along these lines, and they are the people who have since been most effective and faithful in Church life, and have, in almost every case, pursued extremely interesting and worth-while careers in industrial life. It seemed that here was an effective instrument ready to hand, and it was very widely agreed in Church life that this movement was a "good thing". Yet it was only put into action in half a dozen parishes up and down the country. However, perhaps it is only fair to add that the essential point of Jocism and kindred movements is that the whole structure of a man's working and domestic life must be spread out before God, and caught up into the action of the Eucharist. This was seized upon, and emphasized, by "Parish and People" and the liturgical movements in England and on the Continent.

An Industrial Community

In the shipyards, engine works, and factories in Pallion, the vast majority of the working people live in Sunderland, and up to comparatively recently it was possible for a great many Pallion people to walk to and from work, and even get back home to dinner. Although Sunderland will shortly have a population of nearly a quarter of a million, it is still a fairly tightly knit community, in which people know one another very well, and is not a merely loosely knit conurbation, as the boroughs are on Tyneside. This makes it possible for the parochial clergy to make ready contact with the works, and to be accepted as such within the local set-up. It may be that, in some respects, North-East England is not as starkly secularized as some other parts of the country, so that the vicar of the parish is still accepted in this kind of way.

The ecumenical issue has not been directly raised, but within the works there have been extremely friendly relations with people of the various Christian communions, and this has been especially true of a number of extremely able and thoughtful Roman Catholic shop stewards.

Within a shipyard or factory the parish priest will be doing work that is essentially pastoral in character and in intention, yet, as with the fulltime industrial chaplain, he will, of course, exercise exactly the same kind of care to avoid any kind of proselytizing.

The parish priest, like the industrial missioner, if he remains in the same place over a good long period of time, is able to get together groups of people who are prepared to meet and discuss, outside of working hours. These will not be large groups, but they can be very interesting, and, whether they are largely active trades unionists, or whether they are groups of personnel managers, it can provide a meeting place between those who have been working all their lives in the old industries, and those who have recently come into the area in the new industries on the Trading Estates. The parish priest ought to make a point of getting to know those who work in the Youth Employment Service.

It emerges very often during the discussions with those who are concerned that only a small minority of industrial workers are prepared, on behalf of their fellow men, to persist in the kind of sustained effort that is involved in the work of a shop steward, or other such official. They are often genuinely devoted people, and in need of encouragement in face of frustration and disappointment at being let down so often by their fellow men. Their work involves a ministry by the minority, *vis-à-vis* the majority, who appear to them to be quite irresponsible, and interested only in "money, pools, and pints". The clergy are not the only people to indulge in lamentations. Perhaps some mutual encouragement may ensue!

The Parish Priest and the Christian Worker

It has constantly been asserted by those engaged in industrial mission that the parish church ought to exercise the kind of self-denying ordinance that refuses to tether the more intelligent and responsible sort of church-going industrial worker to the parish pump. He must be free to give of his best, as a responsible person, to the Trades Union movement, to the Town Council, or to his professional association, and the parish priest ought very readily to agree. The truth of this kind of assertion is more generally recognized to-day than it used to be. At this point, however, it is important to state that, if the influence to be exercised by the responsible worker in the secular world is to be effective and sustained, it is essential that he be rooted and grounded in a firm apprehension of the Christian faith, and in a deep knowledge and love of God and of his fellow men. Experience suggests that, although a man ought not to be tethered to the parish pump, yet, if he is to survive effectively as a focus of Christian influence, he will need a strong sacramental life as the background to his existence. It looks as though the Roman Catholics do much more for the spiritual life of the industrial worker than we do in the Church of England.

The parish priest who has worked for a long number of years amongst people in industry becomes hesitant about accepting some current generalizations. It is not true, here in Sunderland, that there are very few church-going Anglicans who work in our local industries. In the largest of our shipyards and marine engineering works there are a substantial number of people who play a leading part in church life, and are exercising some kind of responsibility of a worthwhile sort in industrial life, at very varying levels.

It is often said that the clergy must be willing to learn when they enter into industrial life. What use can be made of this learning? If it leads to a real understanding in some depth, then a parish priest is better equipped for training and guiding young people who are about to become apprentices. The Church today is weak in the kind of moral theology which enables apt advice to be given, spiritually, to an industrial worker, and a sound working knowledge of industrial life is a great help here, as it is in teaching and preaching where a man's ministry is in an industrial setting. He must use his knowledge responsibly and with integrity especially in any situation where he can be of use in a work of reconciliation. This will not often involve him in any overt negotiations within industrial disputes. In these days suspicion and misunderstanding go very deep; this has worsened in recent years. Any work that is of a healing sort needs to be done at a pretty deep level. It is only viable where the priest is selfless in doing it and where any sort of publicity is avoided.

Strains and Stresses in Industrial Life

In the early days of industrial mission it was assumed that the bulk of the work would be directed towards encounters with manual workers on the shop floor. In these days manual workers are a much smaller proportion of the total labour force employed in a large factory, and there is no doubt about the fact that men who work in many different kinds of supervisory grades, along with technicians, and middle management in general, are very deeply perplexed, sometimes driven almost to despair, by the apparently insoluble nature of the problems which they meet almost every day. Awareness of this, of course, does not suggest that the need could be readily, or quickly, met by the parochial clergy, but it does suggest that the parochial clergy need to be more fully aware of the kind of strains to which men and women are subjected today, in their working lives, and, at the same time, to realize how radical a change has come over the pattern of working life, at almost every level, during the last twenty-five years.

It may be that the parish priest is able to visualize a good deal of what goes on in industrial life, without being too closely involved in it. He is aware of the immense importance of their working lives to industrial men; yet, in many ways, work means far less to industrial men today than it did twenty years ago. He is able to see the same man both at work and in his domestic setting, and this will prevent him from arguing too hotly about the real work of the Church being *either* in the parish *or* in the factory.

Of course, there are dangers and drawbacks, as full-time practitioners know only too well. There is a sense in which a parish priest can do only a mere fraction of the work that cries out to be tackled. There is the appalling problem of the rapid mobility of the parish clergy in these days; and the parish priest knows that a great deal of this kind of work is intimate, intangible, and personal in character. He knows that his successor may not be at all at home in this kind of field, or he may be succeeded by someone who will rush in and make blunders.

Industrial Mission and the Clergy

The parochial clergy in the Rural Deanery are interested and appreciative of the fact that work is on foot which they value; and yet it is true to say that, over the years, very few have made the kind of contacts in industrial life locally that are open to a parish priest. The shyness and the hesitancy persist, and there is curiously little available in the nature of training offered to the young clergy for this work in most large industrial towns. An outstanding exception is in the thorough training given to the younger clergy who are associated with the training schemes for young miners provided by the National Coal Board in County Durham.

The shyness may persist, up and down the country, partly because of the very widespread impression that there was a wedge driven in between industrial mission and the parochial clergy. There was, earlier, resentment over this, and particularly about the implied suggestion that the parochial clergy were tinkering about with an outworn institution, while the specialist practitioners in the field were getting to grips with the secular world, or with the "real" world. The parochial clergy have tended to identify industrial mission with "South Bank attitudes", and to sheer away from this whole field. This is not the moment to embark on words about "busyness" or priorities. Equally it would not do to indulge in a tirade about the liability of so many parochial clergy to be hamstrung by keeping in being their "organizations". Instead it can briefly be said that a parish priest who is prepared to learn and to listen will find that the work which lies open to him in an industrial setting can, and should, make valid demands on his time. Because the work is done in a field in which the priest is there on sufferance, rather than by "right", it is specially salutary for him. He has to earn acceptance and to maintain this in proving his integrity. This fact alone makes the work worth while for the priest. The work is exacting, but it is both interesting and rewarding. Its direct results cannot be easily assessed or measured; yet, when faithfully maintained, it is essentially fruitful.

The Challenge to Authority

MICHAEL KEELING

We have to deal today with a society that is radically different from any that has ever existed in the past. The reasons for the change are complex and we shall not be able to go into them very deeply here. But many of the effects of the change are obvious, and one in particular will concern us in this chapter. It is the demand which is beginning to be made—and will be made with increasing force in future—that all members of society should have the right to make their own decisions, moral and otherwise. The situation has been described succinctly by Professor Charles Vereker of Durham University in a lecture to teachers involved in the Gloucestershire scheme of education for personal relationships and family life.

> The complexity of an urban industrial society which generates its own pace of change calls for a greatly increased ability on the part of all its members, not only to understand these processes, but to share the responsibility for directing and controlling them. Earlier, more static and only slowly changing communities placed their emphasis on the maintenance of static roles and a fixed social order for carrying out predominantly traditional tasks. Modern society must either submit to strong collective centralization or be ready to incorporate ever larger numbers of its citizens in the responsible duties of democratic living. . . . The problem of education in these circumstances becomes more subtle than how to inculcate a knowledge of the Old Testament commandments; for it is not the proscription of theft which requires emphasis so much as the development of the kind of moral independence of judgement which leads to such an activity being rated as self-evidently anti-social. None of the agencies for moral training in our society, not churches or schools or even parents, are yet alive enough to the different methods and direction of

education in this field, where the emphasis must now be placed on encouraging independence at the same time as developing self-control and social co-operation. The task is not an easy one and, after centuries of following a different model, it does not come naturally.[1]

The problem for Christian education and for Christian mission is that we now have to find ways of dealing with people that will be an adequate response to this demand. The challenge to authority which is implicit in this development of society constitutes not a small change but a revolution. Because the characteristic attitude of mind today is both well-informed (or, among young people, anxious to be well-informed) and critical, there is a danger that it may seem to the established Christian to be hostile or potentially hostile to the Christian faith. It would be a pity if this judgement were to be made and to persist. The contemporary state of mind is not hostile to the Christian faith, but it needs to be properly understood; informed criticism does not do away with authority, but it does demand a different sort of authority from that which has been generally exercised in the past. What it means now to talk of "the teaching office of the Church" (if you happen to be in one tradition) or "the claims of the Gospel" (if you happen to be in another tradition) will have to be worked out over a long period and with some pain; as Vereker points out, it is a process for which we are as yet by no means ready.

In this chapter we shall look at some of the influences which have brought about the present mental, moral, and social climate, and try to see how they relate to the Gospel and to the institutional Church. In Chapter 8 we shall look at some practical ideas about teaching which can be of use in developing in others

[1] "Moral Education in a Changing Society", reprinted in *Education for Personal Relationships and Family Life*, the Second Report of the Gloucestershire Association for Family Life, pp. 29–30. Obtainable from 2 College St, Gloucester. Charles Vereker is Professor of Politics in the University of Durham.

and in ourselves the independence, self-control, and social co-operation which Vereker specifies as the necessary characteristics of the new society and which, as we shall argue, a Christian response to modern society demands.

The Contemporary State of Mind

The characteristic attitude of mind of the present generation is the product of four major influences.

1. The first is the coming of the scientific way of looking at the world: it is true that the "scientific attitude" has been about for a very long time, but it did not penetrate the main body of society until the arrival of mass education and mass communications. The idea of testing the accuracy of a theory by observation, by conducting an experiment, by a survey, or by an investigation of some sort constitutes a standing challenge to all statements about values. Because statements about values (for example, the moral values of the Christian religion) cannot be tested directly by statements about facts (for example, the results of sociological research), we are always entitled to think that something is good even if we cannot prove it; but the scientific attitude of mind has affected the concept of moral authority in two ways. Among many people who are not trained in philosophy, and particularly in the philosophy of science, it has spread abroad the idea that science can answer most things and may one day answer everything; among people who have some knowledge of what modern philosophers and scientists are saying, it has put theology (and ethics and aesthetics) into a tight spot with the questions "What test is there by which we can decide whether your statements are true or not?" and "If there is no such test, do your statements have any meaning at all?"

2. The second influence is the study of psychology. If the activity which goes on below the level of conscious thought can produce effects in the conscious mind which are outwardly quite

unrelated to the subconscious needs and desires (so that, to take one example, the fact that a child commits a theft may be connected with the fact that he or she has been deprived of affection), it becomes less easy to be sure that our ideas about God are not also just products of the subconscious mind. Our ideas about human personality are also being challenged by biological studies, and particularly by the rapid advances in the study of genetics, but this has as yet had much less effect on the public mind than the study of psychology.

3. The third influence is the visible success of the series of revolutions in the social and economic order that have affected all the countries of the west in some degree. At any one moment "socialism" may be more popular or less popular, but there is a general awareness that from time to time a social revolution pays off, in terms of such things as education, social security, working conditions, or civil liberty. This helps to maintain an atmosphere in which the *status quo* is not automatically accepted. On the international level our attitude to communism has been affected by our knowledge of Stalinism in Russia and of the "cultural revolution" in China, but it has been affected also by such matters as the very visible Russian scientific achievements in the space race.

4. The fourth influence is the change in the means of communication that has brought the other side of the world (particularly Vietnam and India) into our living rooms: the mass media, whatever their drawbacks, cannot help carrying a great deal of information about social reality; even at their worst we know that they are reflecting back to us the face of the society we have made. It may appear cynical to say so, but the more we know about society the less respect we are likely to have for those who are running it.

To these four we must add a fifth influence which stands out on its own: the effect of two world wars. These brought millions of people face to face with facts about human nature and human society which can to some extent be avoided in times of peace, and consequently they broke up the respect for the established order which had been almost automatic among all but the poorest classes in Victorian times. They possibly did not create social change, but they certainly hastened it.

These influences have affected different people in different ways and to different degrees, but between them they have had an impact which has made modern society quite different from its predecessors. It is not possible to be very precise about this change, but over the whole range of people, from the executive to the butcher's boy, from the Young Conservative to the hipster, there is discernible a modern style of mind which is characterized by such words as "questioning", "sceptical", "permissive" and "cool". It does not, of course, include everybody. Against it is ranged on the one hand the romantic Left, believing strongly in its own vision of the workers' state, and on the other hand the romantic Right, believing equally strongly in its version of the British (white, English-speaking?) Commonwealth, short hair-cuts, and compulsory church-going; and there are many minor variations on both themes. But if one were to investigate the mental attitudes of the whole British population, I guess that one would find that the majority of people share to some extent in the main attitude of mind described above. This is not a merely British phenomenon: it is an international style of mind, which is as recognizable as international typography or international hotels, and which stretches in the same way in varying degree from London to Tokyo and from Moscow to New York.

Some readers—perhaps particularly some of the clergy—may be saying to themselves at this point that this is all very well if one is talking about the intelligentsia, the sort of people who live in Hampstead or Bayswater and read *The Guardian* and *New Society*, but that the situation is very different in Little Saltmarsh-under-Water. If so, they could be mistaken. When the Little Saltmarsh butcher's boy stops coming to church eighteen months after his

Confirmation he does so, among other reasons, because he senses
a dissociation between his daily life and the life of the Church
which arises in part from the influences we have described above
and from the failure of the Church to take sufficient account of
the changed society in which it is living. The fact that he is
unable to express this feeling in words does not mean that he does
not experience it. Many people live by the Christian faith for
reasons which they would be quite unable to talk or write about
at length but which are none the less valid for them, and the
opposite is presumably also true.

One particular result of all these changes has been a loss of
faith, not so much in what Christianity stands for as in the expression of it through the institutional Church. Colin Hickling
has already commented on this situation and on the figures for
church-going and for religious belief in England, particularly as
analysed in David Martin's study *A Sociology of English
Religion* (see "Worshippers Occasional and Lapsed", above,
page 1f). Martin's figures suggest that on the Sunday of the
Religious Census in 1851 about 36% of the total population of
England and Wales attended church (roughly 16% Anglicans,
16% Nonconformists, and 4% Roman Catholics), while on the
results of various recent polls about 15% of the total population
of the whole of the United Kingdom attend church on any one
Sunday now (dividing into about 5% Anglicans, 5% Roman
Catholics, 1·5% Presbyterians, 2·5% Free Churches and 1%
others—including 0·2% synagogue attenders).[1] The two sets of
figures are not strictly comparable, being based on different
areas and arrived at by different methods, and as Martin points

[1] S.C.M. Press and Heinemann Educational Books, 1967, pp. 19 and 43.
The two main modern surveys referred to by David Martin are "Television
and Religion" (see note 3 on p. 8) and a survey taken by National Opinion
Polls for Ronald Goldman ("New Society", 27 May, 1965). The interpretation of the figures from the Religious Census of 1851 is quoted by Martin
from an article by Dr W. S. F. Pickering, "The Religious Census of 1851—a
useless experiment?", *British Journal of Sociology 18*, 1967.

out the present-day figures probably err on the generous side, being based on claims to churchgoing rather than on counting at the churches. But even as they stand they show a substantial drop in the number of people attending church on any one Sunday. On the other hand, a large number of people still claim religious belief of some sort: the survey *Television and Religion* which was undertaken by Social Surveys (Gallup Poll) for ABC Television in the London, Midlands, and Northern ITV areas, showed 84% who claimed to believe in a God of some sort (including concepts of a "Vital Force which controls life"), and 64% who said that they believe that Jesus is the Son of God.[1]

The sociological factors which influence our attitudes to religion, such as age, sex, social class, increased physical, occupational and social mobility, and regional variations in Church affiliation and attendance, are at least as important as the factors we have discussed, but it would be outside the scope of this chapter to deal with them adequately; the general point that seems to stand out from sociological studies is that the non-religious factors may together be more important than the religious factors in determining general religious practice (though not, of course, in determining the religious practice of specific individuals).

The possibilities of deduction from such facts are endless. But if we restrict ourselves to the argument about the mental climate of modern society which we have been following so far, the point which is of outstanding importance is the growing tendency to independence of judgement and the way in which this change is being reinforced by the trend in education towards a more child-centred, permissive, and inductive approach. Education is becoming an affair of dialogue rather than monologue, and through it more and more people are going to be helped to be open-minded and independent. This is the fact with which Christians have to

[1] University of London Press, 1965. Paragraphs 163, 175, and 180.

reckon. We are going to have to revise our ideas about the teaching authority of the Church and about the claim that the gospel makes if we are to deal effectively with people in today's society. The contemporary mind is not willing to take anything crudely on authority.

The Image of the Church

Christians, and the churches to which they belong, by failing to observe or take seriously the change in the mental climate have earned themselves the reputation (however undeserved) of not being very interested in truth.

> "Of course," she said easily, "there is a quality of life in Birkin which is quite remarkable. There is an extraordinary rich spring of life in him, really amazing, the way he can give himself to things. But there are so many things in life that he simply doesn't know. Either he is not aware of their existence at all, or he dismisses them as merely negligible—things which are vital to the other person. In a way he is not clever enough, he is too intense in spots."
>
> "Yes," cried Ursula, "too much of a preacher. He is really a priest."
>
> "Exactly! He can't hear what anybody else has to say—he simply cannot hear. His own voice is too loud."
>
> "Yes. He cries you down."
>
> "He cries you down," repeated Gudrun, "and by mere force of violence. And of course it is hopeless. Nobody is convinced by violence. It makes talking to him impossible—and living with him I should think would be more than impossible."[1]

Lawrence is here giving a description of Birkin (or of Gudrun's view of him), not of a priest. But it is surely devastating that the image chosen for Birkin should be that of a preacher: ". . . . there are so many things in life that he simply doesn't know . . . He can't hear what anybody else has to say . . . He cries you down." For this is not merely Lawrence speaking: there would be no point in having Gudrun compare Birkin to a preacher unless

[1] D. H. Lawrence, *Women in Love* (chapter 19).

the ideas which are taken from the preacher and applied to Birkin appeal to what we already know of a preacher, so that the image can draw on our own sense of its justness, however much it may surprise us at first. Lawrence is appealing to an idea of the preacher and priest which we cannot entirely disown. If Lawrence's evidence is not acceptable, let us take a witness who is nearer home in time and nearer home in the sense of being himself a practising Christian, and indeed a priest and preacher. Canon Eric James, in speaking to various meetings on behalf of "Parish and People", has said:

> I regularly have to speak at conferences for Sixth Formers. Frequently I put before them a list of various groups of people in society—scientists, historians, sociologists, philosophers, theologians, etc.—and ask them to arrange the list in order of those most concerned with truth. Very rarely do theologians and the Church come out near the top. Most young people think that religion is concerned with a "hand-out" which sooner or later you have to accept—sooner rather than later if you are to do what parsons want.

Notice that this is not evidence from Canon James but evidence which he has gathered directly from young people themselves in circumstances in which they have no incentive not to tell the truth; and that the evidence is that among a fairly random selection of Sixth Formers the priest is not regarded as a leader among those who are looking for truth. This is not a fair image because most clergy, and most Christians, are genuinely concerned for truth, but it is an impression that has been created by an over-anxiety to guard particular definitions of the Christian faith at the expense sometimes of a willingness to listen. It is our willingness to listen which is the measure of our concern for the world. It is willingness to listen which the contemporary world takes as the measure of concern for the truth: in this sense, if Christians are not seen to be ready to listen, they are not likely to be seen as those who have found truth. I suspect that this is one of the obstacles in the minds of many young men who in other days would have come forward for ordination, and that it is also one of the difficulties in the minds of at least some of the clergy who have to go in the pulpit twice every Sunday and attempt to communicate in a setting in which they are completely removed from any possibility of listening as well as talking.

None of this is meant as an attack on the clergy themselves. The clergy are the prisoners of the system they are employed in. Within that system they are generally seen as sincere people, doing a good job, as the survey *Television and Religion* showed.

> The clergy are thought to have the greatest influence for good in the community: 34 per cent of those interviewed put the "priest, vicar, or minister" as the person with the greatest influence for good (paragraph 257).

> Even greater than the proportion who say that the clergy do a lot of useful work (83 per cent) is the proportion who say that the clergy are sincere in their beliefs: 90 per cent say that the clergy are sincere, 5 per cent say they are not, and 5 per cent do not answer the question (paragraph 271).

But it should be remembered what the concept of the work of the clergy is:

> At the personal rather than the political level, the subjects where it is thought that the Churches can be of special help are: the death of a near relative (87 per cent of those interviewed); loneliness on moving into a new district (77 per cent); ill-health (65 per cent) (paragraph 248).

Although the majority of the sample thought that the Churches should be concerned with social questions (paragraphs 239 to 247), it is almost certainly these personal services, rather than any teaching authority, which gives the clergy their good image (see also paragraphs 133 to 162 on the limited ability of religion to influence behaviour). So far as the authority of the Church is concerned, the survey does not support any more optimistic view than we have put forward here.

The Approach to Other People

Let us concentrate on the positive side of these facts. There is one principle that is fundamental to the New Testament and answers directly to the situation of the Christian in the modern world: that the approach of the Christian to his fellow men must be made in love. For example, the First Letter of John, chapter 4, verse 7, reads "Dear friends, let us love one another, because love is from God"; and again (verse 20) "But if a man says 'I love God', while hating his brother, he is a liar". Faith is not much use unless it shows itself in the practical approach of love to our fellow men. The idea of loving our fellow men can cause difficulties because we often use the word "love" in a sense that is foreign to the Bible. The word "love" now often means romantic love— moon and June and love at first sight—but this is not what we mean by "the love of God". We get closer to what the Bible means by "love" when we talk about the love of parents for children, because here the word "love" contains ideas of "guarding" and of "bearing with"; but even the love of parents for children is not a proper analogy for the love of God. The love of lovers for one another and the love of parents and children involve emotion and the physical expression of affection. This tenderness is part of our love and our love is part of God's love. But God does not require us to feel loving towards our neighbour in this sense—at least not to begin with. A better word for the sort of love John talks about would be "acceptance" or "trust". John also says "There is no room for fear in love; perfect love banishes fear" (verse 18), and this is not a passing comment about something that love happens to do: it is a definition of the kind of love we are dealing with. The love of God is the approach to other people that makes it possible for them to be themselves —to be without fear of us or of their own nature. When people say "But I don't feel loving towards my neighbour", they are missing the point. "Loving your neighbour" starts not with a feeling,

5

but with the moral recognition that *whether we like it or not* God accepts all men as they are, and by doing so puts to us the challenge "What is your approach to your fellow men?"

What does it mean to say that God "accepts all men as they are"? Let us take some help from another field of study. As a technical term the word "acceptance" is associated particularly with social service casework. This profession has paid a great deal of attention to the relationship between its workers and its clients, and in one of the standard works on the subject, *The Casework Relationship* [by Felix P. Biestek, S.J.[1] the principle of "acceptance" in casework is defined as follows:

> Acceptance is a principle of action wherein the caseworker perceives and deals with the client as he really is, including his strengths and weaknesses, his congenial and uncongenial qualities, his positive and negative feelings, his constructive and destructive attitudes and behavior, maintaining all the while a sense of the client's innate dignity and personal worth. Acceptance does not mean approval of deviant attitudes or behavior. The object of acceptance is not "the good" but "the real". The object of acceptance is pertinent reality.
>
> The purpose of acceptance is therapeutic: to aid the caseworker in understanding the client as he really is, thus making the casework more effective; and to help the client free himself from undesirable defenses, so that he feels safe to reveal himself and look at himself as he really is, and thus to deal with his problem and himself in a more realistic way (page 72).

There are three points in this that are worth noting for the purposes of our own study.

1. The object of this policy of acceptance is to establish reality: to see clearly the person who confronts us as he really is and to help him to see himself as he really is.

2. Whatever the reality that is revealed, we come to the other person with one judgement about him already made, that simply by existing as a human being he is a person of "innate dignity

and personal worth". This is the fundamental judgement that every Christian is called upon to make about all his fellow men by virtue of their being fellow human beings and by virtue of his being a Christian. It is this judgement that establishes the only condition upon which the other person can be his real self. In casework the individual caseworker presumably relates this principle to whatever system of values he or she holds; Biestek himself relates it to the Christian faith.

3. We accept the other person for what he is, not in order that he may remain what he is, but in order that he may be changed; that is to say, in order that he may learn to change himself. There are two assumptions behind this statement. The first is that all of us need to be changed: the standard against which we are measured is not one that requires some minor improvement, such as would be required by some idea of good citizenship; it is by the fulness of God himself that we are measured (see, for example, the Letter to the Ephesians, chapter 3, verses 14–19). Here again caseworkers presumably relate this need to their own system of values, whatever it may be. The second assumption is that in fact we cannot change other people, we can only help them to admit the need to change and to carry through the change themselves. (In saying this we are not ignoring the power of grace; we are simply concerned to rule out the sort of violence by which we sometimes seek to impose change on other people.)

In practical Christian terms our attitude to the word "acceptance" is of the highest importance: if God takes the Lord's Prayer seriously he loves us only as much as we love people who break up telephone boxes or youths with long hair and noisy motor bikes or men who molest children or people who support another political party from our own. "Love" or "acceptance" in this context has a precise meaning and is far from being a vague affirmation: it means "to desire to help; to desire not to hurt; to see clearly the needs of". As we grow in the Christian faith it may come to mean more than this; but here we begin to move out of the field of moral theology into the field of mystical theology, which is a different matter.

This willingness to accept other people is the basis of our authority in the world. The heart of it lies in the second of the three points above, our judgement about the innate dignity and personal worth of other human beings—all other human beings. For the first of the three points is just the necessary precondition for any action, and the third of the three points is something that may or may not be fulfilled; but the middle point, our judgement about the worth of the other, is the one which shows how much of God there is in us, and which makes it possible for the other to respond to us. If we have renamed "love" as "acceptance", perhaps we ought also to rename "authority" as "the ability to call forth a response". For this is what we are after: not a way of making people conform, but a way of sharing with them what we know to be true.

This "love", this "acceptance", does not rule out the possibility of evaluating what the other does: we can still say—and at times may have to say—to the other person, "Look, this is wrong". Biestek makes this clear with his next principle, which he calls "The Nonjudgmental Attitude".

> "The nonjudgmental attitude is a quality of the casework relationship; it is based on a conviction that the casework function excludes assigning guilt or innocence, or degree of client responsibility for causation of the problems or needs, but does include making evaluative judgments about the attitudes, standards, or actions of the client; the attitude, which involves both thought and feeling elements, is transmitted to the client."[1]

This distinction between "assigning guilt or innocence" and "evaluative judgments" is crucial: it is the difference between saying "You are a bad person" and saying "This attitude or

[1] Op. cit.

action of yours is not helpful/socially acceptable/expressing your real needs". We cannot avoid making judgements about other people's actions (we know whether we approve of the actions or not) and these impressions are bound to get across to the other person: the judgement that we have formed is one of the facts in the situation. But we must not transfer these judgements from the action to the person: that is God's business. It is possible to disapprove an action but still accept the person. It is more than possible—it is necessary.

The moral authority of the Christian lies solely in the fact that he comes to his fellow men knowing that "he who loves God must love his brother also". "Loving" means being prepared to lay a foundation of trust so that there is no fear in any relationship. Until this basis is established there is no possibility of further building and therefore no possibility of progress in the Gospel. All too often, Christians have given the impression of wanting to leave this stage out. On the one hand, with people we fear or resent (such as the "thugs" or "perverts" of the writers of letters to the newspapers) we want to omit the stage of accepting in order to punish and to control; on the other hand, with those who are potentially interested in the Gospel we want to omit the stage of accepting them as they are in order to rush them into accepting Christ—in effect to fill the pews, though this would rarely be a conscious aim of Christian action. Let us make a distinction here. For a particular individual a moment may come when he or she is ready to accept Christ, when a word, an invitation, is all that is necessary to produce the response. To this moment we must always be sensitive. But to suppose that this moment exists in the here and now for all people, and that the refusal to take the step forward can only be wilful disobedience, is to be insensitive to the amount of building that needs to be done, and in particular to be insensitive to the need for the Christian to prove, by the sort of person he is in his relationship with the other, that the gospel is worthwhile. Whenever we omit the stage of accepting the other as he is, without wanting to do anything about him, we commit the mistake of wanting to use him for our purposes instead of his own (a fact which is easily overlooked because of the apparent altruism of our own motives). It is a mistake in terms of the Gospel, because it is for the other *as he is now* that Christ died, not for him as I would like him to be. Let us translate the word "acceptance" back into the word "love": it is the love which Christ has for the other as he is now that we must show.

The Christian has no authority except the impression he makes as a man who lives the gospel. Is he a man who is open, seeking, humble, giving, accepting, a bringer of peace? Or is he a man who is closed, demanding, accusing, fearful, and dependent? Other men see the Christian first of all in relation to themselves. It is in our attitude to others that we are put to a test that everyone can understand.

The Call to Dialogue

What, then, about mission? If the basic approach of the Christian to his fellow man is one of acceptance, of helping him to know himself as he really is and to begin to change himself, does not this fall very far short of what we have always understood by "preaching the gospel"? The answer is no, because this way of mission is more effective than any other, and nearer than any other to what the gospel itself teaches us about other men and about ourselves. The old idea of proclamation was all too often, in Lawrence's words, an attempt to convince by violence. England being predominantly a Protestant country we are well trained to recognize a threat of moral violence in the "authoritarianism" of the Roman Catholic Church, but we have been less well trained to recognize that there is a similar violence in some Protestant preaching and moral instructions: and note that it is the word "preacher" that Lawrence first uses.

St Paul wrote ". . . if the trumpet call is not clear, who will prepare for battle?" (1 Cor. 14.8), but the virtue of a trumpet call in a military context is that its message is clear and its authority is accepted. These conditions are not always present when we come to preach the gospel. It is no good giving a clear lead unless it is done in such a way that people can and will follow. It is the job of Christians to proclaim the gospel and there must be a sense in which this will mean giving a clear lead in a society which otherwise lacks moral leadership. But giving a clear lead means first of all facing realistically the question of the most effective way of carrying out this commission. In spite of all appearances there is a real desire for the message that Christians have to give, but there is not a widespread desire to become a fully paid up, practising member of the institutional Church. Many people who believe vaguely in God and are attracted to the person of Jesus Christ would be very hard to convince that the institutional Church has any connection with their own intimations of holiness. To these people the "giving a clear lead" or "preaching the gospel" in the sense in which these terms are normally used would be as much a barrier to the truth as an opening to it.

If the Christian is to teach now and if he is to proclaim the Gospel he must do it by means of a conversation that recognizes that both sides have a right to be heard: he must be ready to enter into dialogue with other people rather than to preach. It is worth remembering again that the normal process of education is becoming increasingly a matter of dialogue, responding to the changed needs of a complex and rapidly changing society. The aim of Christian engagement in such a conversation will be to express what we ourselves know of the life of the risen Christ —in us and in others—so that others may recognize the same experience in themselves. We do not want to fill other people with information about the gospel or the Church, or to make them conform to a certain way of behaviour, or to bring them to a sudden decision, or even necessarily to change them; rather we

want to help them to identify and to deepen an experience in
themselves. This is the same experience that we know in our
lives, and that we ourselves constantly seek to deepen. All this is
rather different from the way the gospel was proclaimed in New
Testament times, but the New Testament proclamation was
successful precisely because it began where its listeners were,
and we, if we are to begin where our listeners are, must begin in a
different place.

Authority in the Church

What we have said about acceptance and dialogue is as true for
relationships among Christians as for relationships between
Christians and those who are not Christians. The moral independence of judgement of which Charles Vereker writes is as
important within the organization of the Church as it is in
society as a whole. If Christians are to be effective in mission,
they must themselves constitute a community which is both
accepting and engaged in dialogue within itself. The challenge to
authority posed by the contemporary mind is therefore a
question as much for the institutions of the Church as for the
relationship of the Church to the world at large.

There are in any situation basically two kinds of authority:
institutional authority and moral authority. Institutional authority is that which is conferred on one human being by others in
order that he may do a particular job (policeman, chairman of a
committee, prime minister, bishop); this authority is usually
supported by sanctions of some sort (anything from a mild
rebuke to several years in prison). Moral authority is that which
convinces us by its own quality: it operates without the need of
sanctions. Most institutions work on a mixture of these two
kinds of authority. This is particularly so with the Church,
where there exists an institutional authority—the right to cele-
brate the sacraments, the right to exercise oversight—but where
there is also a claim to moral authority, which in the Church is a

claim to the presence of the Spirit who convinces us. When moral authority is connected with institutional authority in this way there are bound to be times when the holders of institutional authority do not in fact possess moral authority. We face an inescapable dilemma: without institutional authority there is the danger of anarchy, but with institutional authority there is the danger of the dead hand. Because the gospel is about love, about being made new, authority in the Church is empty unless the leader has himself been seized by love. It is essential to have a system of institutional authority in the Church, but it is essential also to have within that system a continuing sense that institutional authority is not enough.

Part of the solution of this dilemma is to be found in the word "democracy". This is a word which raises some hackles when used in the context of Christian institutions, but some words change their meaning slightly when they are put in a Christian context, and "democracy" is one of them. The Christian community is a democracy of the Spirit, which means that on the one hand the vote of the majority is not a final assessment of any question and on the other hand authority cannot be equated simply with hierarchy: the final authority is the Spirit in the whole Church. Leadership is not a permanent possession, for ever given to some and denied to others: within any group it passes from one to another as the needs of the moment dictate. In the Christian community the Spirit is present in all the members and he can and does speak through any and all of them. Whether we are talking about moral authority or about institutional authority the basic process is one of dialogue, of the joint advance by equal partners towards a common goal. It is this authority—or the lack of it—that those who are not Christians can most easily see and understand.

A Contemporary Response

We began by stating three facts about the present situation of the

Church in society: that the modern mind is critical and not given to accepting authority: that there has been a loss of faith, not so much in the gospel as in the institutional expression of Christianity in the historic churches; and that the contemporary image of the Church is that of an institution which is not seen to be looking for truth. These facts could be seen as rather depressing, but they can also be seen to represent a healthy development of the human spirit. The Church has everything to gain from being criticized, as has any human institution. The development of the contemporary mind is a move towards the fulfilment of two words which are very important in the Bible, "freedom" and "love". It is a demand on the part of humanity to be treated with the worth which the Bible gives it: it is, one may hope, a real growing up (though the capacity for destruction within the human race is almost equally great).

The response of Christians to this claim must be first of all to acknowledge its justness. The Church has always been bound to some extent by the social conditions of the time and place in which it has operated, and since western Europe in the past has been a highly structured society the Church has naturally tended to operate in a highly structured way itself: in its major manifestations it has been hierarchical and authoritarian. The rise of democracy in the modern political and social sense has been on the whole a process of growth in respect for other people and a freeing of men from unnecessary constraints. This is bound to have an effect on the Church. It may be, in fact, an opening of an aspect of the gospel previously not sufficiently taken into account either in the organizing of the Church's own life or in its approach to others. Our God is a living God, and living in this world means change. The response of the Christian to the contemporary world should be one of courage and hope.

How does all this help the parish priest, or the group leader, or the youth leader, or the layman who is trying to live out his or her faith in relationships at home and at work?

Let us try to summarize.

1. Nothing that we have said so far detracts from the truth of the Christian message, which is unchanging, as God is unchanging.

2. Our ability to get this message across depends on whether we have received it ourselves and on what difference it has made in our lives. We can make no claim on the basis of the institution we represent or the Book out of which we are speaking: if we do we are wasting our time, which is not our time but God's time.

3. Whether the message gets across depends also on the person at the other end. In particular, it depends on whether he or she finds that the message works. Anyone who wishes to lead, anyone who wishes to proclaim the gospel by word or deed, must recognize and respect the right to independence of those he meets. Our love and our respect for other people must remain the same, whatever their decision. *In a sense we must love people enough not to mind whether or not they accept the Christian message.* In large measure this respect and love are the message.

All this can make the Christian's position a painful one. He has a gospel which seems to him to be of infinite value, and yet he cannot force it on other people: he may have the pain of seeing it rejected. Human nature does not become perfected just by being free. But this is also where the joy comes in. St Paul says "You, my friends, were called to be free men", but he also says "Help one another to carry these heavy loads" (Gal. 5.13 and 6.2). The Christian stands precisely at the point where the strains of life are felt and where others can be helped. His job may seem to be harder than in previous generations because he stands or falls more clearly by the sort of man he is himself; but it can also be more rewarding, because he is engaged with people who really want to know and giving the help they really need.

If in this chapter we have seemed to concentrate on the critical and hostile aspects of the contemporary situation and on the

weaknesses of the Christian and of the Church, it is because the
situation must be assessed realistically before a move forward can
be made. In particular, if Christian mission is to be successful, it
is necessary that the pre-condition of this activity be thoroughly
understood: that the Church has no claim to be heard unless it
goes to men humbly, open to their questions and responsive to
their needs, accepting them freely as they are, in love.

Professors, Priests, and People

BARNABAS LINDARS, S.S.F.

Not long ago a Swedish pastor came to Cambridge and pro-
ceeded to arrange interviews with some of the professors and
lecturers in the Faculty of Divinity, especially those who are
well known to be inclined to be radical in their thinking. After a
few days spent in this activity he returned to Sweden. It may
appear to be a striking admiration for our Cambridge theologians
which could lead a man to come from so far just to meet them
briefly. But the pastor had in fact a practical purpose. His aim
was to gather information about recent trends in Christian
thought, in order to write hymns which would present the faith
in an up-to-date way. It seems that hymns are more important in
the Swedish Church than they are in the Church of England. We
tend to sing the words without bothering much about what they
mean, and provided that the tune is a familiar one we pay no
attention to the bad theology of our old favourites. But they take
them more seriously in Sweden, and they use them to teach the
faith, especially to young people. There was, then, some point in
studying the newer developments of thought for the sake of
hymn-writing. But it still seems strange that the pastor thought it
necessary to come to England in order to do this. His reason for
this was that in Sweden there is such a yawning gap between the
pastors and the theologians, between the parish clergy and the
university men, that he could not hope to achieve his purpose
there. He regarded the professors as experts in their own fields of
study, who could not be expected to have any understanding of
pastoral work. So he came to England, where, he felt, the
distance between pastor and scholar is not so great.

It is comforting that he thought it was worth while to come to this country. But there is a gap here too, which has already assumed dangerous proportions. In all branches of learning there is a tendency towards a greater degree of specialization. The days are gone when one man could be expected to have a high degree of competence in all branches of his subject. In science and technology we have got used to the idea that a very specialized training is necessary. Advances in medicine are usually the result of teamwork by a group of experts, and we generally take on trust everything that the doctor says, without questioning his authority in a field where we feel we have no right to speak. But of course he too has to take it from the experts, often finding it very difficult to keep up with new knowledge and to put it into practice in his medical work. Theology, too, embraces a variety of intellectual disciplines, and the expert in biblical studies can hardly be expected to be highly trained in the philosophy of religion as well. The same goes for Church history, dogmatics, ethics, and comparative religion. In any of these branches of study it is inevitable that the continuing task of acquiring learning should lead to a reassessment of accepted ideas and to the questioning of easy assumptions. But because the subject matter is religious thought, it cannot be brought to the same kind of precise conclusions as the exact sciences, which depend upon observations of natural phenomena. There is always room for a bewildering variety of conflicting theories. This makes it far more difficult for the parish priest to absorb new learning than it is for the practising doctor, and the people are naturally far less ready to take on trust things that they have not the equipment to know for themselves.

This does not mean, however, that there is no contact between the professors and the people. What it does mean is that such contact, when it occurs, can be quite shattering in its effects. The Church in this country has little equipment for very wide publicity, but it is extremely well served by radio and televison. Hundreds and thousands of people can see and hear the professors as they popularize the results of their learning. The parish priest, who one might suppose should be the "middle man" in this process, is bypassed. The professor drops a bomb, so to speak, and when the people tell the vicar all about it, he throws up his hands in horror, feeling that the whole of his ministry is being undermined. He feels that the men in the universities are working against the Church. Especially in matters of faith and morals it seems that they are giving way to the secularists and the humanists all along the line. The parish priest's job is hard enough as it is, without having a stab in the back of this kind. What he wants from the theologians is solid support, as he strives to hold together his flock. Belief and practice go together, and he knows only too well that uncertainty about the faith is bound to be reflected in diminishing congregations and loss of spiritual vitality. What is needed is a boost to their faith and their morals. When the men who should be clever enough to handle all the problems seem to take the side of the unbelievers, then it is nothing less than betrayal. If only they would keep their doubts to themselves it would be a little better, but when they put them into public pronouncements it can only seem like deliberate trouble-making.

If these are the reactions to the attempts that are made to close the gap between the universities and the parishes—and the correspondence columns of the newspapers give ample evidence of them—then it certainly is a situation which demands the most careful thought and attention. We must try to make a closer analysis of the factors that are at stake, and see whether there is some way in which confidence can be restored. Let us look first of all at what the men in the universities are trying to do.

Seekers after Truth

In the first place there is, as has already been pointed out, an increasing tendency to specialization in the academic study of theology. The professors and lecturers are well aware that this is so, and that this makes it much harder to think of theology simply in terms of preparation for the work of the ministry. But they also know that the university is first and foremost an institution of education and research. Pure study cannot be sacrificed to the requirements of vocational training. This is a problem which is, in fact, even more acute in other fields, where, for instance, governments and other interested bodies are liable to dictate the courses of study with a view to promoting their own policies for economic development and defence needs. It is the freedom of the university which is at stake. In the case of theology there is the further fear that any restriction of the syllabus in order to make it "relevant" will reduce the standing of theology by comparison with the high standards required for other intellectual disciplines. It may be remarked in passing, however, that the problem of over-specialization, with its inevitable tendency to seal off one area of thought from another, may perhaps right itself, if such schemes for more balanced syllabuses as those being tried out at Keele and York prove to be successful. But the point I want to make here is that the issue is not just a matter of too much specialization, but the much more fundamental question of the status of theology as an academic subject. The task of the professors is the promotion of learning and the pursuit of knowledge. The vocational aspects of religious education are the work of the theological colleges, just as medical students go to the teaching hospitals and intending teachers take the Diploma in Education

It is clear, then, that the academic theologians are not primarily engaged in building bastions of orthodoxy for the benefit of the Church at large. Nor do they live in ivory castles, exempt from the problems that confront the Church. They are working over their subject in the light of new knowledge and new patterns of thought in the ferment of the intellectual life of the university. Their work demands the same honesty and integrity as any other branch of scholarship. This means that they must approach their subject with a deep sense of responsibility. If this is true of their work in the university itself, it is also true of their attempts to disseminate knowledge to the wider public through popular writing, broadcasting, and public lectures. If the clergy feel that these are too often irresponsible and destructive, it is because they misunderstand what is at stake. In fact the theologians are seeking to support the clergy, not by putting a rubber stamp on an obsolete presentation of Christian faith, but by facing the actual challenges of the day. They bring to this task the same sense of responsibility and intellectual honesty as they give their own work of research and scholarship.

Why, then, are their pronouncements so often apparently negative, and even tinged with a suspicion of unbelief? Here we must be willing to make some allowances. The professors are human, like everyone else. They cannot be expected to be immune from personal doubts as they make the adventure of faith. Moreover the nature of their calling requires that they should have an enquiring mind. They are trained to ask awkward questions, and if they did not do so they would never be able to advance knowledge. When such doubts and questions are shared in public it is not necessarily irresponsible, for they are only bringing to expression the difficulties that are already under the surface of the minds of people in general. It is not good enough to complain that it would be better to let sleeping dogs lie. The difficulties will come out in the end, and it is far better to air them sympathetically and constructively than to suppress them and try to imagine that they do not exist. The accusation of irresponsibility can only be made if there is clear evidence of what I may call a "retreat from involvement" on the part of a theologian. This retreat from involvement occurs when a man chooses the study of theology, not as a vocation within the total life of the Church, but as a *substitute* for Christian commitment. This may perhaps be observed in the fact recently noted, that the decline in the number of ordinands has not been accompanied by an equally large decline in the number of students reading theology at the university. But even here it is dangerous to assume that this phenomenon (which may well prove to be short-lived) has anything irresponsible about it. It reflects rather the pervading uncertainties of the present generation of young people.

As far as the theologians are concerned, I do not think that the accusation of retreat from involvement, with its concomitant tendency to superficial, provocative, and brash public utterances, can be maintained. Nor should we fasten too much attention to the negative aspects of their pronouncements, and forget the great value of the positive aspects. There is real gain when people know the facts about their religion and have the capacity to speak with some authority on matters which are liable to be mis-construed through sheer ignorance. A great deal of good work is being done to create an informed public opinion. It does not catch the headlines like the more provocative statements, but it should be recognized gratefully by those who are quick to criticize the experts.

Audience Reaction

The fact remains, however, that offence is often given, even if the theologians may be acquitted of trying to make trouble and working against the Church. This seems to me to be due mainly to a failure of imagination on their part. They do not always realize that what may be said without fear of misunderstanding to a university audience can give a very different impression to those outside. One of the most obvious examples of this is the use of the word "myth", which really ought to be banished from popular religious discourse. It has become almost a technical term amongst theologians for the expression of timeless truth by means of a story, which may be actually historical, but need not be so. In the hands of the Bultmannian school it serves the useful purpose of making it possible to retain the value of a story, even when the historicity of it is in doubt. But for everybody else, whether clerical or lay, it simply means a story which is not true, a product of the human imagination which is not to be treated seriously. Nowadays many theologians are aware of the dangers of using this word, and take pains to avoid it in popular writing. But it will always be extremely hard to assess audience reaction correctly in advance, when the world of the university differs so greatly from that of the common men. It is not an insult to people's intelligence to take care to explain carefully any technical expressions that have to be employed. On the contrary, to fail to do so runs the risk of giving the impression of intellectual snobbery, which is naturally resented.

We must now take a look at the parish priests, and try to see why they feel so badly let down. The first reason that is likely to spring to mind is the complaint, frequently made, that the clergy simply never open a book from the day when they emerge from their theological colleges. It is said that a priest's year of ordination can be guessed by looking at the range of books upon his shelves. It contains little or nothing published since that date. Such a sweeping generalization is grossly unfair. It is literally impossible for the average parish priest to keep up with all the new books in the midst of unending claims on his time and his energy, which make him far too exhausted for deep mental concentration even when he does make the time for reading. In spite of this, many of them do make valiant attempts to keep up to date, and value the help that is provided by diocesan clergy schools and deanery study groups. If they have managed to keep up some reading, they are, of course, better equipped to sustain the shocks of professorial public pronouncements. But they are still liable to be upset by them nevertheless.

A more convincing explanation is to be found in the delicate nature of the pastoral charge. It is the effect on the people which really bothers the parish priest. He has the task of holding together, and seeking to extend, a congregation of perhaps two or three hundred in the midst of a seemingly godless parish of several thousand. He fears that their confidence may be shaken, and that they may give up the struggle. Moreover he is probably nursing a few people on the fringe, whom he hopes to bring into the life of the church. It is precisely these people who are most likely to be put off by the appearance of uncertainty or contradiction in what they hear or read. Most clergy find their level, and formulate their approach to people and the way they present the faith, in the early years after ordination. It is based on the kind of teaching they have received in their theological college and on their growing experience of their parishioners and of discovering how their minds work. Thereafter it is not likely to change much. There is naturally a tendency to maintain this approach, and a certain resistance to new patterns of thought, especially as these often appear at first sight to be merely destructive. The priest finds himself conditioned to trying to keep his people immune from new trends, which they may find upsetting. And of course, the more successful he is in doing this, the greater is the shock to them when radical ideas reach them through the press and radio. When they come to him waving a newspaper with the latest controversial statement splashed across the headlines, he feels rather in the position of a nursemaid who has to soothe a frightened child.

As far as the people themselves are concerned, the reaction is likely to be more complex. There are some who have always had a simple and unquestioning faith, accepting uncritically the teaching that has been given to them, and disliking (if not actually fearing) any manifestations of religious controversy. All they want is to be soothed down, to be reassured that there is nothing to be worried about, and to have authoritative encouragement to carry on exactly as before. These are very often the most faithful and loyal members of the congregation, and it is obviously important that they should be dealt with sympathetically. But it may well be considered a mistake just to soothe them down, as

will be suggested below. Others are alarmed if there is a contradiction between what the priest has been teaching and what the
professors are saying, and begin to feel that the priest has been
hiding things from them—which, indeed, he may have been
doing to some extent, though with the best motives and without
any intention to deceive. No amount of explanations will really
restore confidence. They feel in a muddle, and do not know
where they stand. If they are well inside the life of the church,
they will probably weather the storm eventually, provided that
they are not overwhelmed by further shocks too quickly. If they
are fringers, the damage may be lasting, and like the disciples at
Capernaum they may withdraw. But there are still others for
whom the radical statements, upsetting as they are, really come
as something of a relief. For it is their own doubts and questions
that are being voiced. Now they really know that they can speak
what is in their minds. Instead of feeling bound to suppress their
hesitations in the presence of the vicar, they can hope to find in
him a sympathetic understanding, for their own difficulties have
turned out to be precisely those which are exercising the minds
of the intellectual leaders in the church.

Priest and People

It is just at this point that the lack of confidence between the
theologians and the parish clergy is likely to lead to failure. The
professors may be doing a lot of damage by lack of wisdom in the
way they present their material, but they are concerned with real
issues and are fighting on the intellectual front-line of the Church.
Those clergy who have sought to seal off their people from
current trends are more likely to have succeeded in rendering
themselves incapable of understanding what the professors are
about. It is clear that the great need is for the clergy to make the
effort to do this. Instead of reacting violently, they need to give
the theologians credit for having a serious and responsible
purpose in what they are doing. On this basis they can try

patiently to discover what this is by going beyond the headlines and thinking carefully over what has been said. It is not good enough to reply that there is no time to do it, for the pastoral task cannot be adequately discharged if these issues are neglected. If the real difficulties of Church people are being brought to the surface, as I have suggested, they need to be able to talk to the vicar openly about them, and they will regain confidence if they find that he is aware of the problems and willing to think them through with them. There may be no simple and straightforward answer that he can give them, but this will matter less if he can at least show some sympathy and some understanding of what is involved.

The effort of understanding is also a help from the point of view of those who are liable to be harmed by discovering a contradiction between the priest's teaching and the statements of the theologians. It is not to be expected that every priest will agree with what is said, or that such contradictions can be eliminated. But a priest who is alive to the issues under discussion will naturally take them into account in giving his own teaching. This will help to reduce the shock when contradiction is felt, and also build up some measure of confidence that it can be coped with successfully without loss of integrity. Indeed it may well be that in some issues the priest's own teaching is not so helpful for someone as what appears to go against it, and it may be necessary to agree to differ. But if so, it can be done with mutual respect and goodwill. Confidence is maintained, and so the chief cause of damage is removed.

If the priest is making an effort to understand what the theologians are saying, he will also be in a better position to help the faithful who only want reassurance. They can be shown that these statements, provocative as they may be, are part of the larger task of building up the Church and maintaining the faith in an age of questioning and uncertainty. Their own fidelity to what they have received is thus part of the same process, though it serves a rather different function. The army on the front line cannot hope to win, if there is no solid support at the base camp. Instead of being worried and unhappy about what is going on, largely because they do not really understand it, they can accept the fact that it happens, have at any rate some idea of the necessity and importance of it, and know that they are contributing *to the same end* by their loyalty to traditional orthodoxy and their faithful church membership. In fact in the present phase of this century, which is subject to rapid developments and fluctuations in numerous walks of life, sheer stability on the part of churchgoers has a vital contribution to make, not only for the continuance (or even survival) of the Church, but also for the good of the community as a whole. There can thus be a positive approach to the bewilderment of churchpeople which can give new purposefulness and vitality to their outlook.

It may seem as if all the onus of dealing with the situation has been placed upon the parish clergy, but this is inevitable, because they have to bear the brunt of the impact. And of course, as they deal with their people, they have to deal with themselves. If they are asked to give the professors credit for integrity, they must be completely honest with themselves as well. One great temptation for the clergy is to shrug the whole thing off with the observation that the various brands of "new" theology are not really so new after all. It is true that almost all the ideas which hit the headlines have had a place in someone's writings at least fifty years before. But there is something that has changed in between. The answers which satisfied people then don't seem to work now! It is not enough, then, to look up the old lecture notes, because they are geared to another context. It is the present situation which is our concern, and it certainly cannot be met by attempting to live in the past.

A Spiritual Revolution

What is it, then, which has happened to make so much difference?

Those who have exercised a pastoral ministry for the last twenty years must surely know what it is. A revolution has taken place in the consciousness of the people. Formerly it was always possible to assume that the idea of God and of the things of the spirit *meant* something to people. There was a recognizable point of reference in their minds. It may have been disregarded, or it may have been explained away as something else, but it was usually there. Most people knew what it was to pray, even if they only did it when driven by great stress. Most people had a vague sense of guilt about not going to church, even if they felt that they could not bring themselves to do so. Then in the late nineteen-fifties something happened. Somehow, and without anything happening consciously, the sense of God slipped away from people's minds. They began to discover that the idea of God was no longer real to them. A variety of factors can be suggested which may account for this change. It was a time of material prosperity and (almost) full employment, producing the feeling that man's satisfaction and fulfilment are to be found in the present, against the "other-worldliness" of religion. Secular humanism was advancing, even making a bid for recognition as a substitute for religion. Serious philosophical objections were being put forward against the possibility of belief in a personal God, and these had widespread popular repercussions, which came to a head later in the *Honest to God* debate. At any rate, since then God has not been a really meaningful concept to many people. This is very easily seen when a person begins to turn to the Church as an enquirer. He can understand a lot of it, but he is likely to remain mystified for a long time by ideas that are connected with prayer, especially when people talk about listening to God and loving God. It is sometimes quite agonizing to see how a most willing newcomer to the life of the Church remains unsure of himself at this point, and feels inferior to the other members of the congregation, and there seems to be nothing that one can say to help, because one has no way of speaking which does not presuppose that point of reference in the mind, which in his case does not exist. Only perseverance and patience and sympathetic encouragement will get him through.

But the revolution did not only happen among the unbelievers and the uncommitted. Everyone has been affected by it, though probably not so much among the older generation. There has been a dissociation between belief in God and the sense of reality. People find it harder to feel in themselves the relevance of what they profess to their understanding of life. This is why so many feel muddled and unhappy. Their difficulties cannot be solved in quite the same way as they used to be. A new theology is required, not because the truth about God and his revelation of himself in Christ has changed, but because man's apprehension of these things has changed. It is precisely at this point that many of the theologians and professors are speaking. This is why it is so important that they should be given a sympathetic hearing. But the unfortunate thing is that the language that they use is often so misleading. A phrase like "religionless Christianity" can be very much to the point in this discussion when it is properly understood. But it is only likely to lead people deeper into the morass when it is used as a slogan, a sort of short-cut to avoid circuitous explanations, which (like so many short-cuts) can easily come up against a dead end. The phrase depends on a definition of "religion" which was current in Bonhoeffer's Germany, but it has never had that sense in this country. Similarly "man's coming of age"—another phrase derived from Bonhoeffer —belongs to the revolution of thought of the present century, describing as it does the emancipation of man from the necessity of feeling dependent on a divine force outside himself. But it does not really describe the revolution which is the point at issue here. For Bonhoeffer it was a liberating thing, freedom *for* God, not freedom *from* God. It was not meant to imply that man had "grown out of" the need for God, or could ever do so.

The Rediscovery of God

The point is that the urgent task for man today is to rediscover God within himself. We are back with the Deism of the eighteenth century if we put all the emphasis on the external objectivity of God. If we cannot find him within ourselves, we cannot find him at all. This is, indeed, recognized by contemporary theologians. But even here there is a pitfall. There is a theology, voiced by American writers, but based on German existentialist philosophy, which goes to the other extreme, and denies the existence of God apart from ourselves. The slogan of this school is "the death of God". Here is another dreadfully misleading phrase, which is culled from Nietzsche, but is a parody of what he meant. To him it was a liberating idea, as he saw man shackled by the "big man with a stick" notion of God, which he knew to be utterly false. Delivered from such a crippling concept, man could be free to be himself. To the new theologians it means dispensing with the idea of God as object, so that the search for God becomes indistinguishable from the effort for self-understanding and self-realization. To the man in the street it would appear to mean that religion is over and done with, but these theologians are closer to Nietzsche than that. They think of it as a liberation from the despair of doubt, as the existence of God is no longer something that has to be proved. But in fact it is only likely to lead to despair, as men find, not God, but themselves. In this predicament what man needs is the revelation of God as it is given in the Man Jesus Christ. The gospel remains supremely relevant to those who would assert that "the proper study of mankind is man".

Of course it *is* very trying and difficult when such emotive and confusing phrases are used. But it only shows how urgently necessary it is to keep the lines of communication open between the theologians and the main body of the clergy and people. There is a closing of the gap to be done from both sides. The theologians need to pay far more attention to the dangers of misunderstanding in their public utterances, and the clergy need far more patience in their attempts to assess what is being said. There must be—as surely there is—integrity on both sides, and there needs to be a corresponding willingness to place confidence in one another. The problem of the Church in the twentieth century is not due to superficial things, like changing the hymn-tunes or clinging on to dreary services, or any other of the thousand and one "reasons" which people give for "not going to church". It is due to the revolution in man's inner consciousness, and it has to be tackled at that level. New expressions—and, let us hope, not misleading ones—will have to be found to make the "faith once delivered to the saints" immediately meaningful and relevant to man's understanding of himself, so that he may know himself both as a creature made in the image and likeness of God, and as one transformed by the renewal of the mind to put on the new nature, created after the likeness of God in true righteousness and holiness. Perhaps, like our Swedish friend, we shall one day have hymns to sing which say what we really mean.

The Perils of Biblical Preaching
BARNABAS LINDARS, S.S.F.

Though the days are gone when a missionary would arrive with nothing but a Bible in his hand, the Bible still remains the basis of preaching in most churches. It is still customary, more often than not, to begin the sermon with a text. And the text is generally chosen from one of the lections set for the service, whether it is the Eucharist or Mattins or Evensong. It used to be said that one could twist the text into anything you wanted to say, as if it were just a peg to hang your own ideas on. But on the whole preachers today disapprove of this, and with good reason. They pay careful attention to the meaning of the whole passage from which their text is taken. It is the message of the Bible itself which they want to put across. The sermon is closely related to the passage on which it is based, and at the same time it is geared to giving positive help, inspiration, and guidance to the congregation. This is the great tradition of Christian preaching, seen at its best in the homilies of St Augustine, the works of Luther and Calvin, and the sermons of John Wesley. The last twenty years have seen a great revival of interest in the Bible, most notably among Roman Catholics, who had formerly tended to use dogmatic schemes as the basis of homiletic instruction. But now the Bible has been reinstated as the book of the faith, not as a textbook of dogmatics, but as the record of the central facts which form the historical basis of Christian belief and practice. The unique position of the Bible remains unchallenged.

It would be gratifying to say that all this is to the good, that we have a welcome return to the historic centre of Christianity, and a new confidence in the abiding value of the Bible as the inerrant Word of God. But this is not the case. There are factors arising from the increased interest in the Bible itself which tend to undermine confidence, and these can present difficult problems to the preacher. He is not immune from these difficulties, so that he has the double task of sorting out his own position and working out what is the right thing to say to his congregation. And if there is a serious chasm between what he thinks in his own mind and what he says when he is in the pulpit, the people's confidence is likely to be shaken all the more, besides the unbearable tension which he has to suffer himself.

The chief source of difficulty is the fact that the Bible cannot be taken simply at its face value. Most people realize this to some extent, and would not regard themselves as verbal infallibilists. On the other hand, lacking the equipment to unravel the knots of this extraordinary collection of religious literature, they tend to be quasi-fundamentalists, taking at face value the bits that they do understand, and not bothering about the rest. This means that they leave out nearly the whole of the Old Testament altogether. And because they know that various things are questioned in it, they feel free to reject what does not fit in with their own ideas. On the other hand, as they study the Bible more closely they begin to be vaguely aware that it does not quite fit with the credal orthodoxy which they have learnt, and so become unsure of their own beliefs. This is not usually to be traced only to private Bible reading, because most people impose upon it their own preconceived ideas, which are usually in line with orthodox teaching. They unconsciously interpret it according to orthodox presuppositions. But when they listen to biblical exposition in sermons or Bible class, given by a priest who has been trained in the procedures of biblical criticism, his own approach is liable to convey this impression. This is specially true of the way of speaking about Jesus in presentation of gospel material. The average unthinking believer tends to over-stress the divinity of Jesus in his unconscious presuppositions, whereas the critical expositor tends to place the emphasis on the humanity

Is the Bible Discredited?

Here, of course, the priest probably has his answer ready. If the people show signs of disquiet at the implication of what he is saying, he can embark on a lecture in biblical theology. It is precisely at this point that the questions begin to come on thick and fast. He cannot speak along this line without supporting his position with a vast apparatus of interlocking results of biblical criticism. It is clear that he does not take the Bible at its face value at all. The explanation may show that he has a consistent position, but it fails to be convincing, because it is really more than the people can take. They are left bewildered by it all. The net result is the feeling that we can't believe anything definitely at all. Some will dig their toes in and decide to discount everything that he says, and return to their traditional orthodoxy and quasi-fundamentalist attitude to the Bible. Others may remain confused and unhappy, unable to go forwards or to go back. Their uncertainty is not helped by the fact that some of the results of biblical criticism are in any case now so widely canvassed, and yet so little understood, that there is a certain feeling that the Bible is in some sense discredited.

The spread of biblical criticism has been done not by the churches but by the schools. In Church teaching the critical approach may be there in the background, and so preparing the way for the uncertainty which I have just described. But the clergy have no wish to talk about it directly, unless they are driven to it, because their first concern is to teach the faith and to encourage their people to live Christian lives. In the schools, however, specifically religious aims necessarily have to be avoided, and the teaching mostly takes the form of scripture knowledge. It is bound to be a more literary and historical approach. Teachers can hardly be blamed if they try to make their exposition interesting and convincing by including some of the so-called "assured results" of biblical criticism. Children find the naturalistic explanations of miracle stories illuminating and helpful, without necessarily feeling that they are any the less acts of God. But of course they are now equipped to discount them when they reach the stage of questioning belief in God altogether, which they tend to do when they are still too young to assess the Bible theologically. Similarly they may well be given some simple introduction to the Synoptic Problem, which is not in the least intended to undermine their faith. But in the long run they carry away the idea that Matthew was copying Mark, and Luke was copying Matthew and Mark, and (possibly) Mark invented it all. In other words, the value of the triple tradition, which many children (and adults) feel to be the strongest proof of the veracity of the Gospel story, has been undermined. In this way the feeling that the Bible is discredited can grow up without any intention on the part of the teachers, who are doing their job conscientiously and responsibly for the most part.

So the popular mind about the Bible hovers on a knife-edge. On the one side there is a near-fundamentalism and a strong wish that it might all be true. On the other side there is scepticism about the whole thing and the feeling that a few more discoveries like the Dead Sea Scrolls will prove that the Church has got it all wrong and been completely misguided from the start. The newspapers have got this exactly right. Every now and again they give space, under a sensational headline, to some new theory which purports to solve all the riddles of Christian origins. These articles, however different they may be, always run true to type. They are compounded of literal acceptance of the purely factual elements in the Gospel record, disbelief in the orthodox interpretation of it, and some new archaeological or literary discovery which is supposed to throw light on it. These are then worked together with great ingenuity to produce a case which appears to be unanswerable. It is useless for the scholars to complain that the whole construction is untenable, because it is based on faulty presuppositions. These articles, like all successful journal-

ism, are geared to the popular mind, which does not understand
what biblical scholarship is really doing.

Biblical Thinking

Evidently, then, there is a task to be done in the way of dissemina-
tion of sound biblical scholarship. But at once it will be objected
that the pulpit is hardly the right place to do it. A study group, or
a short course of lectures with discussion, might offer a better
opportunity. The more serious members of our congregations
might be induced to take part in this sort of thing, and in fact
there are often very valuable results gained when it is undertaken.
But I now want to suggest that these things need to be taken into
account even in the pulpit. The sermon brings together the
devotional, liturgical, act in which the people take part with the
practical application in Christian living, at a time when the
greatest number of them are gathered together. Although people
quickly forget sermons, the impression of what is said remains as
a formative influence on their outlook. If the sermon is con-
structed in an arresting and challenging way, it is often remembered long afterwards, in spite of the fact that it soon passes
from the surface of the mind. Some facts sink down into the inner
consciousness, and are available to be recalled when people are
faced with difficult questions.

It is in fact this long-term formation of the mind which we
are really aiming to do in our preaching. The whole job of
creating a Christian community—a parish where people feel that
common worship is the vital centre of their lives, and where
Christian attitudes flow from it to inform their approach to the
world in which they live, so that they may bring Christ to bear
upon all secular situations—depends on the formation of a truly
Christian mind. The new emphasis on the Bible at once suggests
that biblical thinking is the most important ingredient of this.
We want our people to think theologically, and we know how
extremely rare this is. If we consider our lay people of best

quality, and try to analyse how it is that they seem to have "got something" which marks them out from the rest, in nine cases out of ten it will be this particular mental grasp. On the other hand we cannot be content to assume that such a mental grasp depends entirely on a person's intellectual and educational qualifications. Christianity is intended to be the religion of the common man, and we have to take care to make it so. Biblical thinking has to be conveyed in palatable and assimilable form at the point where people are most open to receive it. Their liturgical worship (which is a thing they should *enjoy*) and their practical expressions of the love of Christ (which they should *feel* to be vitally relevant) need to be explained in biblical terms and theological categories again and again, so that they may gradually acquire a Christian self-awareness, and feel that they really know why they are doing these things.

Our plea, therefore, is not for the use of biblical scholarship simply in order to correct popular misconceptions. It is the larger aim of training the people in biblical thinking as a central factor in their spiritual formation. Obviously it is not going to be sufficient to do this in an academic way. We do not want disquisitions on "biblical thinking" as such. Like Christianity itself, it will have to be caught rather than taught. All depends on the handling of particular Bible passages, when they turn up in the lessons and are selected for exposition in the sermon. An episode like, for instance, the Feeding of the Multitude, which occurs in the Sunday Gospels three times during the liturgical year, may be much loved by the people, but belongs really to the category of stained-glass windows. When expounded in the light of biblical studies it springs to life with an immediacy which at once makes it relevant and meaningful.

Preaching the Feeding of the Multitude

It will be worth while to consider this example in a little more detail. It is easy to imagine the problem which this episode can pose to the preacher. He knows that the form-critics have laid all the emphasis on the transmission of the tradition within the context of the early Christian eucharist. He has an uncomfortable feeling that the miraculous element in it has been grossly exaggerated in the course of transmission. He is not at all sure what actually happened, because the process of development has inevitably obscured it to a considerable extent. He does not want to pour pure scepticism from the pulpit. The easiest thing to do is to take it as it stands, retell it with the aid of a little vivid imagination, and draw from it a practical moral or spiritual lesson. This is not in the least to suggest that it may not be a good sermon, or that the point made may not be both valuable in itself and a valid interpretation of the Gospel story. But it remains open to the dangers which have been already indicated, and not least the lack of conviction that may result from the tension in the preacher's own mind between what he is saying and what he really thinks about it.

Let us see, then, what happens if he takes the people into his confidence, and expounds it from a critical point of view. He may begin by drawing attention to the circumstances in which the story was *remembered* by the early Christians, who after all did not preserve everything that Jesus said and did. This is obviously the eucharist, and if the sermon is being given in the course of Holy Communion it will be a simple matter to put the congregation into relation with the primitive communities of Christians among whom the story circulated. From here he can point out that much of the language of the story reflects the details of the eucharistic celebration, just as in the case of the similar language in the accounts of the Last Supper. This can be done in a vivid way, which conveys the note of authenticity and engages the attention of the hearers. A distinction has now been made between the form of the story and the underlying tradition. The form of it at least, as an anecdote in primitive eucharistic homily, can be seen to have its own intrinsic worth and credibility. The people thus already have something of positive teaching before them, without being required to take the story simply at its face value. Indeed they can at this point be warned that it would be a mistake to take it at its face value, for that would be a failure to treat the material according to its true character. Another point that can be usefully introduced at this stage is the fact that differences between the four Gospels (not forgetting the second Feeding miracle found in Matthew and Mark) may be partly due to different emphases in the manner of celebrating the eucharist at different places. This implies that the other evangelists are not simply "copying" Mark, even if they base their narratives on his, but that other influences are at work in their handling of the tradition.

After this positive approach to the form of the story, with its realistic (and therefore to some extent self-authenticating) attitude to the complexity of the transmission of the Gospel traditions, a certain degree of uncertainty or prudent reticence about the underlying episode will be neither shocking nor unexpected. Certainly it will be needful to assert that a real incident lies behind it, for to dismiss it as fictitious would be as unsound as to take it literally without regard to the factors that have gone into the making of its present form. But the question which needs to be asked, and laid before the people at this point, is what Jesus was intending to teach when he fed the people in this way. The answer to this question cannot be extracted from the tradition by itself, but depends on the general impression of Jesus' teaching as a whole. As the most constant characteristic is the proclamation of the near expectation of the Kingdom of God, with the aid of a broad range of eschatological ideas and imagery, we are probably not far wrong if we interpret the miracle in terms of an anticipation, or actual foretaste, of the messianic banquet, which is a symbolic way of describing the joy of the coming era. It is perfectly possible to put this in a simple way, without actually using such technical terms as "eschatological", which people cannot be expected to understand.

After this has been done it is an easy matter to draw together the threads, so that the actual incident, the forming of the tradition in the primitive eucharist, and the act of worship in which the people are engaged, are seen to belong together, and the whole is closely related to the essential teaching and redemptive work of Jesus. The realism of the approach can have a truly liberating effect. Many of their unspoken queries have been answered by the way. The preacher is clearly being honest, and knows what he is talking about. Doubts which may be felt about the story when taken *au pied de la lettre* are dispelled by the constructive use of form-criticism. The disquiet felt because of a vague knowledge of the Synoptic Problem has been allayed by the positive attitude taken towards it. Whatever attitude may be adopted towards the miraculous element in the story (and I do not want to suggest for one moment that it has to be denied), the incident has been removed from the category of the stained-glass wonder-story, and has been set firmly in the context of the redemptive activity of God. In other words, the people have been brought within the orbit of biblical thinking, and the training which is so necessary has been begun.

Moreover, in this case we have by no means exhausted the possibilities of fruitful biblical preaching. The Johannine interpretation offers further lines of exposition which are closely related to the Church's understanding of the Christ event. There are hints of the Passover, the theme of the Manna in the Wilderness, and above all the assertion that to eat the bread is to assimilate Jesus, who is the Word of God. Any of these themes can be used in preaching with a frank avowal of the special character of the Fourth Gospel. People are helped rather than hindered by the knowledge that the Johannine discourses can hardly be taken as verbatim reports. The important thing is that such commonplaces of critical scholarship should be imparted in a constructive way. There may be justification for shock-tactics in the pulpit in some circumstances, but this is not one of them. The shock has already been felt by people through the sensational reporting of biblical theories in the press. What they need to discover is that biblical criticism is not shocking after all. On the contrary, it is, as we have tried to show, both illuminating and helpful, if used judiciously.

Honest Reserve

And this is the real difficulty for the preacher. How hard it is to embark on the perilous course of purveying biblical criticism in sermons and to succeed in doing it judiciously! It was a shrewd comment when one parishioner remarked that the new curate had to "work off" his college ideas to begin with. It would be a fatal mistake to unload biblical criticism in the pulpit as if it had any special virtue in itself. There was a famous occasion when the speaker at a training weekend for Sunday school teachers gradually discovered that his lecture was virtually meaningless, because they had never been initiated into the mysteries of the pentateuchal symbols J, E, D, and P. He then set about teaching them all about them, because he could not establish any communication without them. Needless to say, confusion continued to reign among the teachers, and the point of real communication was never reached. If such symbols are in use, it implies that there is a common stock of knowledge, and that an abbreviation or technical term can immediately conjure up the whole range of related ideas in the minds of the listeners. This can never be done in a sermon. Technical terms need to be avoided, or at least explained every time they are used, if they cannot be dispensed with. However many times the same material has been used, it is necessary to assume no knowledge at all on the part of the audience. Each sermon in which biblical studies are used should be complete in itself, as if the congregation were hearing it for the first and last time. But this does not at all mean that *everything* has got to be crammed into each sermon—far from it! It is desirable that it should contain as little as possible, only that which is actually necessary for the matter in hand.

Work that properly belongs to the study should be left in the study. We may, if need be, refer to the interweaving of strands of tradition in the Pentateuch, and to do so may be both illuminating and liberating for the people. But there is no need to bring in the Four-Document Hypothesis to do so.

Greater difficulties can be caused by the extremely speculative nature of much biblical scholarship. All the positions which were formerly regarded as assured results have been questioned in recent years. Biblical studies are like scientific hypotheses. They are always provisional, and may have to be revised in the light of further research and new discoveries. It is not possible for the parish priest to keep up to date with everything that is going on. Fortunately a great deal of work has been done to popularize the findings of biblical scholarship, and much that has been done will be long lasting, even if it must still be regarded as in some degree provisional. Theology is not a quickly moving subject like the sciences. For the purposes of preaching it will be necessary to speak a shade more definitely than strict considerations of accuracy might allow, otherwise it would defeat its own ends by becoming too complicated. The preacher will, then, have to maintain a certain reserve, and be ready to tone down his statements if occasion demands. It will not be difficult to show that the function of preaching requires the exercise of a reasonable degree of licence. The important thing is not that he should know all the answers, which in any case is impossible, but that he should base what he says on what he believes to be true. He knows that the last word has not been said on the subject, but this is the way he understands it according to such knowledge as he has.

In this way there can be a real easing of the tension that can exist in the preacher's mind between what he really believes and what he feels bound to say for the good of his people. But it will not necessarily be done away altogether. His private views may be so extremely radical that it would only be destructive to air them in sermons. Here too there is need of due reserve. Very radical views are as speculative and as provisional as any other theories. If the preacher remembers this, he will realise that he must often make a choice between possibilities of equal merit. The fact that the exigencies of building up the congregation demand that he should choose a possibility which he does not himself prefer, does not mean that he is being dishonest. As the servant of Christ, his function is not to preach himself, but to preach the gospel. For some, then, a tension will remain. But because it is assessed realistically, and the provisional nature both of the views that are expressed and of those which cannot reasonably be expressed is recognized, it will not have a damaging effect. The preacher will know what he is doing, and will not be so uneasy in himself as to undermine the confidence of others.

The Personalism of the Biblical Message

It is precisely to build up confidence that it is so important to bring the results of biblical scholarship into the scope of Bible exposition in sermons. If it is an error to presume on people's knowledge, it is equally a mistake to underestimate their intelligence. Many of the uncertainties which they feel with regard to the central tenets of the faith arise from the loss of the sense of the supernatural in the face of the advance of secularism. This is not altogether a bad thing, as too much emphasis on the supernatural in religion easily slips into quasi-magical and superstitious ideas. Of course it can hardly be claimed that the Bible is free from such presuppositions—that is scarcely to be expected in such a vast assortment of ancient religious literature. But biblical scholarship has shown very clearly the radical personalism of its central message. The characteristic biblical categories are not impersonal and automatic, but such ideas as promise and fulfilment, ethical demand and response, reverential love and obedience. God is found in human situations rather than in external pressures from a transcendent order of being. The incarnation is, in Johannine terminology, the *sending* of the Son of

God, all of a piece with the sending forth of the word of God in the act of creation and in the mission of the prophets of Israel. The special genius of Jesus' teaching on the Kingdom of God is the personal immediacy of his message, so that he creates in the hearer an inescapable confrontation with God himself, who meets him both with judgment and mercy. So closely is this woven into his own mission as the proclaimer of the Kingdom, that the response to his preaching is indistinguishable from the response to himself. In the language of traditional evangelical piety, the teaching of Jesus compels the "decision for Christ". In the Pauline understanding of the apostolic mission, the Christ-event is appropriated by the response of faith. The utterance of the word of God, which was spoken "in flesh" in the person of Jesus Christ, continues in the apostolic preaching to bring the truth as it is given in him to bear upon contemporary life and society, both in judgment and in mercy.

The biblical categories thus provide a third alternative in the midst of the uncertainties of a time of transition. Or rather it would be better to say they provide a constant which remains valid in spite of the existing tension. The realism which is gained from a form-critical approach to the Gospel comes about precisely because it is based on an attempt to think it through in terms of real-life situations. It therefore brings the personal element to the fore. On the other hand the language of angelology and demonology, etc., can be seen to be part of the general presuppositions of the thought-world of the time. Our changing thought-world may have to revise, if not to discard, some of these elements in the biblical picture. This can be done, because they do not touch the core of the biblical material. On the other hand this ought not to be done in a destructive way. There can be acute difficulties at this point. Unfortunately it is the great festivals, Christmas, Easter, and Whitsun, which placard such unacceptable presuppositions most prominently. At Christmas, at any rate, most people seem to be able to suspend judgment for the time being, and swallow everything whole for the sake of goodwill. But this is at the cost of an almost complete dissociation of their religious ideas from their normal understanding of life. A destructive approach might be felt to be necessary, as the only way of breaking out of this intolerable situation. But, as I have already remarked, shock-tactics are not really helpful, and in the circumstances of festival preaching can be positively hurtful. If, however, the preacher is aware of the personalism of the essential biblical message, he will know that there is something to be said which is valid for both worlds. He can move within the setting of the story as it has been given in the tradition, and make it relevant and meaningful to the realities of life in the present day.

The message of the Bible is not only valid for the world of New Testament times and for the new era in which we live. As the word of God it remains valid for all times. "All flesh is like grass", says the prophet of Isaiah 40, "and all its glory like the flower of grass. The grass withers, and the flower falls, but the word of the Lord abides for ever." And St Peter, quoting this passage, adds: "That word is the good news which was preached to you." God, creation, prophecy, incarnation, redemption, and apostolic mission, confront man through personal address, the utterance of the divine Word demanding the response of faith and hope and love. The preacher today stands in the same line of the continuous utterance of the word of God, bringing it to bear upon the particular people committed to his charge in a particular time and place. The message of the Bible is God speaking to man, but it is to be spoken to man as he is now. The renewed interest in the Bible must not be allowed to lose its own object, by becoming merely an archaic or nostalgic return to the well-worn pages. The inner meaning and vitality of the Bible must be made accessible through competent and clear-headed exposition, as well as through commitment and dedication to its message. Biblical preaching has its dangers and its difficulties, but it is central to the pastoral craft.

Reading the Bible Today

COLIN HICKLING

"I treat the scholars as I treat the lawyers", said a distinguished
Anglican when presiding at an international congress of New
Testament researchers. "I listen to what they tell me, and then
do what I have already decided." The incredulous gasp of the
visitors from the continent was not echoed by the Anglican
clergy present. For it represented too well the view that most of
them had, more or less unconsciously, always held. Technical
discussion of the New Testament is a game, played with its own
rules, one in which you can score points or lose them. For the
most part it is a game in which the ordinary working Christian
and his pastor need take little interest. So the enthusiastic participant in a recent New Testament meeting who announced to a
friend that he proposed to give a kind of skeleton *compte rendu* of
its proceedings in the following Sunday's sermon was, no doubt
very properly, rebuked for naivety.

The attitude is easy to understand. If you look at the titles of
articles in a current number of a learned journal, you are unlikely to feel that their contents, even if you could decode them,
would interest you very much. It is not so much that your Coptic
might be rusty, or that lengthy discussion of short passages as
they are reported in, let us say, three different service-books of
the Greek church many centuries ago, might fail to appeal to
your sense of what the Bible is about. The lack of interest, and
the more far-reaching lack of confidence, which the working
parish priest feels in these matters (and with which Fr Barnabas
has dealt in the previous chapter) rest on deeper causes than
this. We may look at these in a little more detail: what obstacles
prevent the priest or layman who feels he stands outside the

charmed circle of the experts, from attempting to appropriate the findings of those within? Having briefly discussed these, we may go on to consider the nature of the positive contribution he may expect them to make.

Pedants or Prophets?

First and no doubt gravest lies the fear, underlined earlier in this book, that these men are demolition experts. They stand with picks and shovels in front of buildings that have been valued. A man who had spent a lifetime in Bible study was outraged recently to discover the opinion that Christ may have been a year or two old when the Wise Men travelled from the East to bring their gifts. How fortunate for his peace of mind that he did not listen to television, still less read the *New Christian*. He might discover that most of those who are professionally concerned with St Matthew's Gospel would assume as a matter of course that there were no wise men anyway. There must be many for whom the demolition of the Christmas story must be as painful as the proposal to deal in the same way with that of the empty Tomb at Easter.

The point here is not so much the truth or falsity of what is being said as the intention detected behind those who say it. Pulling down, rather than building up—pulling down to the exclusion of building up—may be felt to be the real purpose of many of these "godless pedants" who earn their living by teaching the New Testament. And who can doubt that there are occasions when this impression is confirmed? Some teachers of theology seem to hold the view that to shock and scandalize is a uniquely effective educational technique. Use of the mass media may have a similar effect.

Secondly, there may too be the feeling that the concern of the New Testament scholar is with the dead past. The inquisitive third-year physicist who picks up a theological journal in a library might well discover, for instance, a discussion of St Paul's teaching at some point in relation to a phenomenon called gnosticism. The young man concerned might be excused for assuming that this movement was something belonging wholly to a closed and extremely remote period of time. A conscientious priest, anxious to "catch up" with his New Testament studies, might find a great deal of space devoted in books and articles to the early Church's confrontation with contemporary Judaism. He might reflect, with a sigh, that this hardly helps him much with a parish (say in East London) where a sizeable section of the population are orthodox Jews. There would be good grounds for seeing some New Testament researchers as, very properly, having their noses close to the ground, or to the dust, of the first century, and pursuing with great diligence the quest for slightly greater certainty about the events and ideas behind the slender body of primary texts. There would be good, though as we shall see less good, grounds for turning away with the assumption that this has very little to do with the Church of the twentieth century.

The Importance of History

On the face of it, then, an impassable and icy crevasse separates the New Testament specialist from the non-specialist who wishes to live by the Bible in the twentieth century. In part, this must be so. And yet we cannot do other than hope to find bridges, or at least look for bridge builders at work. Fortunately our search is not disappointed. For, on the one hand, a good deal of New Testament study is bound to be historical. The New Testament comprises documents of Church history, and the historian's job is to discover as accurately as he can what the past was like. Its lessons for the present are not his concern, at least not professionally so. Rightly, then, the research thesis in New Testament studies is concerned wholly with the first century, and if a chapter is added relating the findings to the twentieth, that is a more or less gratuitous addition. The facts deserve investigation in their own right. No conclusions can be drawn from them, in any case, until they have been established as accurately as the evidence allows. Many of the differences between one version of the Greek New Testament and another (indeed by far the greater number of them) have no material bearing on the sense. But the textual scholar, as a scientist, is professionally committed to the establishment, as far as he can, of which is the more likely to have been the version written by the author. Only within the context of a reliable judgment over all the details, however small, can trustworthy decisions be made in the few really crucial cases. And in any case, the researcher's dedication to truth stands in its own right. Or again, the date of St Mark's Gospel, within a matter of a decade or so, makes little difference to our interpretation of its value for us today. But the scholar is committed to the attempt to speak with as well-supported a confidence as he can in proposing the date he intends to work with.

But, on the other hand, the New Testament is more than a set of historical sources. As such—to put the matter another way— the personal religious commitment of the researcher is of little or indeed of no significance. The questions put to applicants for teaching posts in New Testament studies, whether written or orally at interview, rightly include nothing about their religious standing. Jews and atheists have as much right to study these documents as Christians, and to earn their living by doing so; and their findings may be—and in the case of Jewish scholars, have frequently proved to be—of the greatest value. Yet the New Testament is also, to quote the title of a study by the German scholar Marxsen,[1] the book of the Church. These writings are *holy* scripture. They have been *canonized*: that is to say, they have been given authority by the Church (not all at once, and in the course of a process which leaves us with a good many questions,

---

[1] *Das neues Testament, Buch der Kirche*, Gütersloher Verlag 1966.

as Marxsen has not been the first to point out.) They form a *canon*
or norm of belief. And they are works which, for the most part,
carry intrinsic and even perceptible authority in their own right.
They witness to Christ: to Christ risen and exalted, and to some
extent to Christ in the days of his flesh. And they witness uniquely.
Everyone knows that there are other documents, some of them
little, if at all, later than some of the New Testament works,
which also claim to treat of Christ and to witness to him. But
these apocryphal works witness in a way that, to a greater or
lesser degree, manifestly is not authoritative. They speak of a
Christ who is far more different from the Christ we read of in any
of the New Testament books, than is one portrait in those books
from any other. (For the witness to Christ of the canonical New
Testament books is by no means uniform.) The canonical
twenty-seven books of the New Testament are the book of the
Church. They witness uniquely to him who is the life of the
Church (rather than, as politicians and others like to put it, to
the Founder of Christianity; though properly understood that
expression also is true).

"*Understandest thou what thou Readest?*"

The New Testament, then, is the book of the churchman; the
book of the bus-conductor (whether ordained at Southwark
Cathedral or not) as well as of the Professor at Heidelberg. As
such, it remains part of what the Reformation established as the
open Bible. When it is half-seriously denied that, in the age of
critical scholarship, this Reformation principle still holds good, a
point is made which deserves attention. But the denials themselves would meet a deep-seated and instinctive resistance. They
are made on the grounds of the unintelligibility of much of the
Bible as read without some background knowledge; of impressions gathered from a bedside reading of the Authorized Version
which may even be misleading. Certainly "rules of life" which
advocate daily Bible reading without insisting on the use of notes

may well be called in question. The Jerusalem Bible, with its introductions and notes, exemplifies a better principle. It is hardly too much to suggest that the whole religion of a regular Bible-reader with little background information will be radically different from that of an intelligent person who has pursued, say, an "A"-level religious education course on the New Testament. Here lies part of the problem facing many first-year ordinands approaching the theological and critical study of the documents from a background of piety little influenced by current biblical scholarship. They are apt to be unsettled, in a way that is absurdly unnecessary, by the raising of questions which have long been accepted as part of the debate. The Church should not have left them innocent in these respects. In a world of increasingly diffused higher education, an adequately instructed Christian ought surely to be able to use his Bible with something of the historical sense—though not of course with the detailed expertise—of the professional scholar.

What Fr Barnabas has said above about the preacher applies, then, to many in the pews as well. Indeed, it is prudent for preachers to remember that Colleges of Education may sometimes be more successful than the Theological Faculties and Colleges in communicating a critical view of the biblical documents. Since the teaching profession has in the past supplied no negligible part of the average Anglican congregation, it may well be that, in this section at least, the desired state of affairs is already coming to be a fact.

Why is this single aspect of a Christian's training being so heavily laboured? To a great extent, for the best of reasons. Jesus Christ is the centre of the Christian religion, the fountain-head of this way of prayer and behaviour. Christians cannot rest content with third- or fourth-hand accounts of this Man who is for them what their faith asserts that he is. They must come as near to the sources about him as they can. They must be as good historians in this regard as their time and opportunities will permit. The New Testament documents are ones which they must know, and know how to use. The point is frequently made that ours is the "God of History". He is the God who acts. This is as much the assertion of the Old Testament as of the New, and in some ways more centrally asserted there. The particular moment in the past at which he did so act—whether it was the Exodus, for the people of God under the Old Covenant, or the Resurrection of Christ for the people of God under that same Covenant renewed and completed—remains the focal point of our religion. No one who has participated either in the Jewish Passover or in its most complete Christian counterpart and fulfilment, the Easter Vigil, can fail to be deeply aware of that. The particular historical past event, we believe, disclosed God to us. To that past event, therefore, we constantly turn our attention, both in our devotion to the God there disclosed in his power and his powerlessness, and in the theology which buttresses devotion and which elucidates and communicates its basis.

Professor Barr is right, no doubt, to warn us that this recent concentration on the acts attributed to God in history must not obscure for us his self-revelation through words as well (the words of the prophets, of the holy traditions, of the Lord, of the apostles). But a point similar to the one already made must still be pressed. The words were spoken in particular contexts in the past. Particular sorts of men (and sometimes women) heard them in particular circumstances. The words are not spoken directly to us. We hear them correctly, realistically, only as echoes from that particular situation. Even for the New Testament period itself that would have been true. Marxsen puts it vividly;[1] what would the church at Thessalonica have made of Galatians? It would have said a great deal to them—but largely because they would have realized it was *not* primarily addressed to them; they

[1] Op. cit., p. 56.

would have understood it in terms of the special needs it was written to answer. We must do the same.

Bridging the Communications Gap

And so we must turn to the main issue: what are the proper questions with which the Christian of today ought to approach the New Testament? How may he put himself in the way of appropriating the wide areas of new light thrown on this work by the scholars? What bridges have already been built across the crevasse separating the lecture- and seminar-room from the house-meeting? What bridges remain to be built?

The first question is the simple and basic one, is Christianity true? The reaction of most clergy and lay people to this can be predicted. This is a silly question for us to ask. We should not be reading the Bible at all, we should not be where we are, if we had not long ago found the answer to this. A reply could be made again to the objection in terms of the very words "long ago"; though it would not necessarily be the strongest reason for this particular approach to the New Testament. There must be still only a small number of people who became Christians as a matter of intellectual persuasion. No doubt this is less true now than it would have been a generation or so ago. But, if true at all, it is a potential source of weakness in a Church which has to cope increasingly (in those who are, as well as those who are not, its members) with varying degrees of latent or conscious scepticism about the intellectual respectability of the Christian position. Many people, no doubt, could illustrate the power of preaching and speaking of less formal kinds which is able to draw on an experience of atheism or agnosticism which was rejected deliberately and on intellectual as well as other grounds. Such witness has for everyone, but especially for those uneasily aware of a faith which has not seriously been questioned, a force and authority which they do not often encounter. What is the "cradle Christian" to do about this? A period of rejection of Christian faith cannot be clinically induced, and it would obviously be from most points of view a shocking thing to attempt to do so. It would in any case be a gamble which might have the least desired results. But at least it is surely necessary to consider the case against Christianity in some depth. Only in this way can the answers provided by Christian apologetic be weighed and, in differing proportions, appreciated as answers to real questions. Theological education in many cases does too little to enable or to encourage the student to appreciate the actual questions and uncertainties which form the present context of Christian preaching. Our Roman Catholic brethren (and this is in some cases as true of the laity as of the clergy) display in controversy a vigour and assurance which are not always glib, and this no doubt in some measure stems from their being much better orientated towards the situation in which apologetic must be skilfully and effectively carried out.

For the strengthening of the Christian's own faith, then, as well as for the sharpening of his effective communication of this faith to the unconvinced, he will need to be familiar with the groundwork of the rational case for Christianity. He will want to work through it with patient sensitivity to the real problems left at every stage for those more reluctant than himself to be convinced. This applies, clearly, at every stage of the argument, from the Christian doctrine of God onwards. The popularity of the Cambridge lectures ultimately published under the title *Objections to Christian Belief*[1] indicates that some younger Christians, at least, are aware of this need.

"Is Christianity true?", then, is a question to be faced seriously for our own good, as well as that of the non-members for whose sake, as Archbishop Temple reminded us, the Church exists. And the New Testament is one of the places where we must do this. Here are the documents which have been used to prove, for

[1] Constable, 1963.

instance, that Christianity was invented by St Paul, or is a variant of Mithraism. Indeed they still are so used, and in a way that now reaches far more eyes and ears; the eyes and ears of people who in many ways are only too willing to be told these things. The remark of a young typist living in Stepney will not be untypical. She thought that scholarship had proved that Jesus could not be the Son of God. In particular, no one watching television can be unaware nowadays of the debate about the Resurrection of Christ. The danger that Church members, as they listen, may misunderstand how this debate bears on Christian belief in the exalted and glorified Lord known by faith, is only a greater reason for reflection and reading. Those who have never doubted the main affirmations of the Creed need—each according to his capacity—to have thought through the basis on which they are founded.

How valuable, then, is such a book as Professor Moule's *The Phenomenon of the New Testament*.[1] Here the fundamental issues underlying Christian belief about Jesus are raised and examined with great thoroughness. The Resurrection itself is the first of these. With patience and rigour, the possible interpretations of the evidence available are examined, and the Christian solution that a decisive objective event took place is pressed home with great skill and persuasiveness. The non-Christian objector is always very much in mind. Professor Moule goes on to consider carefully the "inclusive personality" of Christ as part of the faith of the earliest Church, attested in the Gospels as well as the Epistles. Thus the basic affirmations of doctrine about the Church itself are investigated with the same rigour as the question of the Resurrection. The issue of continuity is also carefully discussed—the continuity between Jesus as he really was and Jesus as the Church "theologized" him. The whole book is a very good example of just the sort of study for which there is so

[1] Studies in Biblical Theology, Second Series, S.C.M., 1967.

great a need. Professor Moule takes very seriously the questions
which we may never have put to ourselves concerning the New
Testament—if, that is, we have lived most of our lives inside the
Church's professed faith in the Risen Christ. But they are
questions which may be real, with greater or smaller degrees of
conscious articulation, to our neighbours. And it is necessary that
Christians should be aware of the weight and gravity of the
questions, and of the basis on which answers can be pressed
home.

It is, however, a book that at some points needs translation
into the idiom of the non-specialist, and precisely this is the contribution that the pastor or the teacher, or the leader, say, of an
S.C.K.[1] meeting or a discussion group, must make. Much good
might in some circumstances be achieved by, for instance, a
series of open house-meetings based on the reasoning worked
through in Professor Moule's book. The homework done by the
leader would be exacting. But one would think that it would
justify itself many times over. And there are many other points at
which the same sort of thing could be done. The East London
typist mentioned a few moments ago, for instance, was one of the
many uncommitted readers of articles in the Sunday press not
long ago about the relation between Christianity and the Dead
Sea Scrolls. As often happens, the allegations made in the press
in these contexts were not answered. One was hard put to it to
discover a small book which presented, in language which the
girl concerned could make her own, the very large scholarly discussion about this vexed and important question. In another part
of London, she might perhaps have found her way, or been
guided, into some kind of house-meeting which took the Scrolls

---

[1] The Servants of Christ the King, who meet regularly in small groups
("companies") for common prayer, discussion, and action. Individual companies vary in the extent to which they make use of the Bible in their meetings.
The aims of the movement were described by Canon Roger Lloyd in *Adventure
in Discipleship*, Longmans Green, 1952.

as the subject for a series of sessions. Again, the homework to be done by the leader (whether a priest or a layman) would have been exacting. One would like to know how many groups there have been over recent years undertaking this sort of study; not, perhaps, very many. There will continue to be a need here, and one which can only be met by a deliberate and very careful and rigorous attempt to carry out a hard and fascinating piece of work: the translation of the scholarly debate—in this case, the debate about Christian origins—into a form in which the less well-educated can see the point and also see and follow the arguments in defence of the Christian position. And if some of the clergy are tempted to reply, "Oh, my people aren't up to that sort of thing—they've never heard of the Dead Sea Scrolls", one can quote the retired shipyard worker who said to me recently (in a house in the parish of St Luke's, Pallion) that he had recently been reading a translation of the scrolls in bed.

Adult education groups sponsored by local education authorities do, it is true, offer opportunities for answering this need—or perhaps one should say, for articulating this need and then attempting to answer it. But this needs, surely, to be done on a far wider scale.

Some construction work, then, is being undertaken on bridges to cross the gap between the pew and the lecture-theatre. Many of them are sited at what is in a way the most important sector of all. The facts of first-century history are not so remote from us as we might have thought. For this reason, scholarly research into these facts can potentially touch our situation very closely. The ongoing technical debate about Paul and "pre-gnosticism", for instance, relates immediately to the question whether Christianity as practised by the main Churches of Christendom is a legitimate heir to the Galilean movement or not. No one will suppose that the building of the bridges is easy. Researchers who are more orthodox as far as their belief is concerned have sometimes been less concerned than others to make their work accessible to the many. All the greater, then, is the need for Divinity specialists in schools, and of course for the clergy, to be *au fait* with the debate (at least as reported in periodicals like the *Expository Times*) and to be good mediators—that is to say, good teachers—in introducing the less well instructed into this debate. People are becoming aware, through the press and television, of a debate going on at a serious and well-informed level with far-reaching implications for their own personal faith. But they have neither time nor expertise to follow the debate for themselves. How essential, then, that those who *are* supposed to have time and to some extent expertise, should do their work of reportage and interpretation.

As an example of what may be done, one might instance two courses for clergy and teachers recently organized in the Roman Catholic archdiocese of Cologne, in which recent work on the Bethlehem and Nazareth stories, and those concerned with Christ's Resurrection, was very fully and effectively presented to non-specialist audiences. One would like to see more activity of the kind in this country.

The Jesus of History

What other questions are we likely to have in mind as we open the New Testament? For many of the older members of church congregations, and many of the most devout, one question puts all the others into the background. And (if this is a fair assessment of their position) they are right to see how fundamental it is. "What sort of a man", they ask, "was Jesus Christ?" It is a searching, and in the past it has been an embarrassing, question; as indeed to a considerable extent it still remains. At no point has the "great gulf fixed" between New Testament scholarship and the congregations been so painful. In a famous sentence, R. H. Lightfoot declared that "for all the inestimable value of the gospels, they yield us little more than a whisper of [the Lord's] voice; we trace in them but the outskirts of his ways".[1] The subsequent reminder[2] that this was a quotation from the end of the Book of Job did little to palliate the conclusion that the "inestimable value" of the gospels must be something, in the light of this judgment, rather recherché. For the ordinary Christian, or for his pastor, such an approach to the Gospels as was summarized by this assertion must be self-condemned. And no doubt there was a time when the conscientious theological student worked in a chilly and forbidding atmosphere. A really thorough investigator of the Gospels, he might have felt, must as a matter of course be a thoroughgoing sceptic. Almost nothing might be said about Jesus of Nazareth as a matter of historical fact, except that he died on a cross.

But the clergy ought to be aware that there has been a certain turning of the tide. Indeed one would like to think that all literate Christians, confronted with the old chestnuts in the office or in the pub, should be aware of the changed situation. A steady stream of writing has emerged, and has been made accessible in summary in various places,[3] on the theme of the "new quest of the historical Jesus". This is not, indeed, a turning of the tide in the sense that we can all return with bland assurance to the old positions, and reconstruct a career of Jesus turning at Caesarea Philippi from the Galilean springtime to the mounting hostility which culminated in Holy Week. But it is a turning of the tide in at least one important sense. Work is being taken up in a new

---

[1] *History and Interpretation in the Gospels*, Oxford 1935, p. 225.

[2] *The Gospel Message of St Mark*, Oxford, 1950, p. 103 footnote.

[3] E.g. R. H. Fuller, *The New Testament in Current Study*, S.C.M., 1963, pp. 33ff. See also C. F. D. Moule, op. cit. pp. 43ff; C. K. Barrett, *Jesus and the Gospel Tradition*, S.P.C.K. 1967, pp. 87ff; O. Cullmann, *Salvation as History*, S.C.M. New Testament Library, 1967, pp. 106ff. See also—among many other books that might be suggested—H. E. W. Turner, *Historicity and the Gospels*, Mowbray, 1963. The issues were discussed in full by J. M. Robinson in *A New Quest of the Historical Jesus*, S.C.M. Studies in Biblical Theology, 1959.

way about the intention of Jesus, the ethic of Jesus, the way in which Jesus thought of his own mission. And all these are questions which are of vital importance for every Christian. It is emerging again that the word "Christ" in the creed does not just stand for an almost totally unknown figure—with reverence might one say, a "faceless Man" in Galilee—but stands for a particular personality about whose activity, and even more, his teaching, a certain amount can be said without much hesitation. This being so, it is of the greatest importance that the Christian should know where he stands. Here, too, a work of mediation is necessary for the benefit of those unlikely to read anything very demanding: they are not on that account less intelligent or critical. The degrees of information in the public generally about the Gospels probably vary wildly and are beyond any survey's power to generalize. The present writer recently met in a coffee-bar an apparently quite educated, if rather too adequately refreshed, traveller who revealed a confident assumption that the earliest evidence for the life of Jesus dated some hundred years or so after the crucifixion. He has also had a shorter exchange with another traveller, more markedly under the effect of alcohol, who showed a surprising—and clearly rather regrettable—accuracy over the quantity of water alleged to have been changed into wine at Cana. There is much to be done to enable Christians to understand what they may assert without hesitation as historically well-founded about the earthly life of Christ. As the "new quest" goes on, there will no doubt be "progress reports" available. How desperately difficult it is, but how vital, for the parochial clergy to keep their reading up-to-date.

It remains true, no doubt, that the question "what may we know about Jesus as he was?" will continue to gain from those best equipped to give them only qualified and limited answers. In one field, however, information has recently been forthcoming which is of the greatest interest and which ought surely to be better known by the ordinary non-specialist Christian. This is

the Palestinian background of the synoptic material as it has been
put before us, most notably, by Professor Jeremias.[1] In reading
Professor Norman Perrin's recent book *Rediscovering the Teaching of Jesus*,[2] which makes good use of Jeremias' work in addition to contributing much that is new, one was struck by the
number of points made that would be of the greatest value to the
"man in the pew". One would agree, of course, that a sermon,
and equally a discussion-group of the right kind, are different
occasions from the university extension lecture or seminar. Yet it
remains true that, if the actual existence and teaching of the
"Word made flesh" are at the centre of Christian faith, then
purely informative material about these matters has a very
proper interest and importance for the Christian man or woman
as such. One of the latter agreed with some enthusiasm recently
that more actual information of this kind would be much valued
by the bible-reader, and that for her it would not be a drawback
that there must be qualifications about the certainty with which
some of the proposed interpretations could be offered. Preaching
on the parables ought surely to be unthinkable (so one might
hope) without reference to Jeremias, even though, of course,
there would be no suggestion that the final answer had been
reached. An attempt to expound the parable of the labourers in
the vineyard along Jeremias' lines was recently thought useful as
suggesting an answer to a problem which had always puzzled at
least one of the congregation. In an admittedly rather piece-
meal way, a good deal of material needs surely to be harvested
from the pages of learned journals as being of interest to every
reader of the Bible. Certainly "interest" is only one element and
that a very minor one in the proper response of a Christian to
the preaching about Jesus. We are often reminded that bio-
graphical curiosity is largely absent from the Gospels, and so in

[1] *The Parables of Jesus*, revised edition, 1963, and *The Eucharistic Words of
Jesus*, 1966, both in S.C.M. New Testament Library.
[2] S.C.M. New Testament Library, 1967.

the larger view it ought to be. Yet people *are* interested in them. The popularity of Dr Barclay's books surely indicates this, if indication were necessary; and so, in a very different and less laudable way, does the interest aroused by the question of the Turin shroud. What we can legitimately know about Jesus as he was, and rather more centrally, about the teaching of Jesus as it was originally understood, ought to be vitally pressing questions in the minds of serious Christians. We cannot answer these questions, in all their complexity, with complete certainty, and some remain baffling. But it remains true that the outlines are fairly clear and substantial.

Finding God in the Bible

So far, however, we have considered only a limited number of bridges, even though these are strong ones across which many good and even essential contributions may be patiently conveyed which have a direct bearing upon the inner life of the Christian and upon his communication with those outside the faith. One great area of New Testament study remains to be considered, and at this point for the first time the Old Testament too is fully brought into view. It may be summed up in the one word "theology". What a pity, in a way, that a better word cannot be found.

For the word "theology" has not the best of connotations. On the lips of others beside politicians, it has the connotations of the most futile, as well as the most bitter, of arguments over words. Even in the minds of many of the clergy the word is ambiguous. It stands for all that, most unfortunately, a not inconsiderable number of ordinands leave thankfully behind when they arrive for their ordination retreat.

Yet, in fact, theology is what we stand for. For theology interprets Christ. We aspire, naturally, to render Christ and his redemption effectively present in our own society. We aspire to do so, in these days perhaps a little too self-consciously, through the contribution we may be enabled to make at many practical points to the well-being of the world. With all this we are very familiar. But this redeeming activity of God in us needs interpreting. There is a place for proclamation, even though it may be made in a quieter tone of voice than that word indicates. And the quieter, the more reasoned and personal, the tone of communication, the more essentially it must become one of theology. How rightly the Lutherans refer to their pastors and ministerial candidates as "theologians".

Theology, then, is at the heart of the work and thought of a priest, as in some sense it ought to be near the heart of the layman and the laywoman who wishes to relate faith to the responsibilities of daily circumstances. As Fr. Barnabas has pointed out,[1] we need to "think theologically". And to that extent, we may feel that the professional students of biblical literature have moved nearer to us and not further away by concentrating as much as they have recently done on the theology of the writers and traditions they study. The problem with which their findings confront us is indeed the sixty-four dollar question. A man may be researching on Isaiah or Ezekiel, on the purposes of St Mark and St Luke, on the theology of St Paul or of the Pastorals. He is concerned at bottom with the question, "What, for this or that Hebrew or Christian mind, did it mean to be a Jew or a Christian at the particular given moment?" And that moment may fall anywhere within a long and complex historical development from the turn of the first millennium B.C. (and the theology of the "Yahwist" is among the most impressive of all) to the turn of the first century A.D. We, in our turn—whether as Christians or as pastors of other Christians, for every responsible lay person has the shepherd's role to some degree—are faced with the question, "What does it mean to be a Christian in the twentieth century?" Nothing less than the faithfulness of God himself, the

[1] Above, p. 83.

truth of the doctrine of the Ascension of Christ, and what it means to assert the activity of the Spirit in the Church, are bound up with this issue. What answers can we attempt in seeking to marry these two sets of questions, those of the students of the Bible's theologies, and our own? What light is cast on our own predicament by studying that of those who responded so long ago to "the God who acts"?

What does "Inspiration" Mean?

One solution lies, surely, along the following lines. We are not permitted, as historians, to allow these documents any privilege of such a kind as might remove them from the "torturing" (to use Collingwood's phrase recently quoted in this connection by Professor Nineham)[1] to which it is the historian's job to subject them. Yet when all this has been said, the men who produced them *were* in a position of privilege (which we may well, if we wish to, equate with inspiration). They stood incomparably nearer than we ever can to the event in which God intervened. None of them, indeed, is an eyewitness. Of that we can be fairly sure. We might be compelled to except from that denial some parts of the Old Testament. Even so, we can scarcely feel that the events leading up to David's formation of a united realm of Israel–Judah, or Nehemiah's contribution to the crystallizing around the Holy City of the new way of life which was post-exilic orthopraxy—the two points in the Old Testament at which many would feel we are nearest to eyewitness reports—were such signal acts of God, such spectacularly *given* interventions of the Lord, as the Exodus. And, old and close to the events as the Songs of Miriam and Deborah are, they are poems too short to fall under consideration here. If we turn to the New Testament, the case is clearer; for St Mark is hardly likely, in spite of

---

[1] In his Charles Gore Memorial lecture of November 1966 (published by the Epworth Press, 1967, under the title *History and the Gospel*, p. 4).

the older commentators, to have been the young man who fled away naked[1]—and even if he were, we do not know how much he could attest on his own authority beside the arrest; and whatever truth lies behind the enigmatic claims of the Fourth Gospel to hand on the sealed guarantee of an eyewitness, it can hardly mean that the author saw these things with his own eyes.[2]

No; the privilege was not that of the first-hand eyewitness. But for all that, it is the privilege of those who received the tradition at its starting-point. Professor John Knox[3] has spoken of the Church's corporate memory of Jesus as the surest source, in the last resort, for our knowledge of him. And even though the evangelists stand on our side of the greatest divide of all, the divide between those who knew Jesus in the flesh and those who did not, they lived, none the less, within a community in which this corporate memory was brighter than it could ever be again. They stood, too, nearer than anyone else ever can to Easter: and that not only chronologically, but in the sense that the Easter proclamation, of which their own writing was an explication and reassertion, was one in which they participated in a more fresh and authentic way than we can. This latter point, if true for the evangelists, is even more true of Paul. A similar claim may be made for many of the Old Testament collections. They were preached from within a tradition which owed both its origin and its vitality to the event, or the self-disclosure of God, to which they witness.

But the theology of the prophets, or of the Pentateuchal traditions, or of the evangelists or of St Paul, means more than this. In every case the theology consists of a process of interpretation, of

[1] See the commentaries of, for example, D. E. Nineham (Pelican) and S. E. Johnson (Black) ad loc.

[2] Cf. C. K. Barrett's suggestion about the authorship and publication of the Fourth Gospel (*The Gospel According to St John*, S.P.C.K., 1956, pp. 113f.), and his comments on the authority of the apostolic testimony, pp. 118f.

[3] *The Church and the Reality of Christ*, Collins, 1963.

application, almost of adjustment. We have been shown recently[1]
how the oracles of the great prophets were handed on in circles
which expressed their faith in the continuing value of what God
had said through them, by a kind of "up-dating" of their work.
They amended and expanded those oracles in such a way as to
reapply them in changed circumstances. In an essential way, the
Gospels do the same. Luke, for instance, is claimed to have been
preoccupied with the problem, which was not anticipated in the
earliest days of the Church, of an "age of the Church" which had
begun to intervene as something more permanent, more demanding of reflection in its own right, than a mere accidental interval
before the second coming would have been.[2] Matthew thinks
through the teaching of Christ from the point of view of a situation of tense rivalry between Christian and non-Christian
Judaism.[3] John does something similar, so it seems, in the context of nascent theosophies such as were to blossom into second-
century gnosticism.[4] In Paul we see something very much more
complex and fragmentary; yet here, too, theology means interpretation. Better, perhaps, it means the correction of false interpretations of "what it means to be a Christian in the first century"
by means of true ones. The very writers of the scriptural documents themselves are, in different ways, preoccupied with a
"communications gap": the gap between the situation in which
the disclosure itself took place and the different one—even
though only perhaps decades later in time—for which the disclosure must be interpreted. In this function alone, apart from
other considerations, they give us a lead.

[1] E.g. J. Lindblom, *Prophecy in Ancient Israel*, Blackwell, 1962, pp
278f.
[2] Cf. Conzelmann, *The Theology of St Luke*, Faber, 1960.
[3] Cf. W. D. Davies, *The Setting of the Sermon on the Mount*, Cambridge,
1964.
[4] C. K. Barrett, op. cit., p. 21; C. H. Dodd, *The Interpretation of the
Fourth Gospel*, Cambridge, 1953.

Making the Bible Contemporary

How, then, shall we interpret and appropriate the study of the diverse yet centripetal theologies represented in the two Testaments? How shall we relate statements about what it means to be under grace *then* with what it means to be under grace *now*?

A first and obvious way lies in perceiving the analogies, none of them close and most of them accidental, yet sometimes real analogies, which exist between the situations of the New Testament writers and our own. With Luke, and his concern for the role of the Church, its mission, its continuity with Christ, the situation is perhaps easier for us than it is with Matthew. And yet the "Pelagian" Englishman with his religion of duty is not so far removed from the assumptions about God and our relationship with him that lie behind Matthew: as witness, perhaps, the (not always very well-informed) appeal made from time to time to the Sermon on the Mount. And no traveller by Underground train in London, noting one advertisement after another for some form of modern gnosticism, can fail to see that there still exist analogies with the situation for which St John's Gospel is thought to have been written. In contemporary India, as Geoffrey Paul has shown,[1] the relevance may be much more striking.

But the perception of analogies of this kind will not take us very far. More grave is our need to be sensitive, with a kind of empathy, to the affirmations about God and the world that undergird and empower the proclamation in this case or that. We ponder, for instance, Mark's stark contrast between the divine and human; or Deuteronomy's awareness of the mutual commitment between God and Israel, and his strangely impressive idealism; or the Priestly Writer's preoccupation with holiness in God and in the community. For the Old Testament, a theology

[1] *St John's Gospel*, The Christian Student's Library, Madras, 1965.

of the Bible such as that of von Rad,[1] provides rich material for meditation. It invites us to pray over the situations of God's commissioned community now, in the light of the same community's situations in a very distant past which is nevertheless a human past, lived out in the same basic patterns of human society as our own. Mainly, it is the scale that has changed. The responses of Israel, and of those who formed and articulated the pattern of her prayer, in prosperity and in insecurity, in periods of religious complacency and also of a certain sort of secularization, illuminate the responses which may be expected of the Church today in situations so different yet in some ways parallel.

Max Warren, writing about the work of the preacher,[2] speaks of the present moment as one of exciting opportunity. Not the despairs, but precisely the hopes, of the present moment provide, he thinks, a setting in which the Bible's affirmations about God can be uttered with new relevance, if only the preacher will give himself to the work of interpretation. What he says about preaching is as true, perhaps more so, for the less formal but more penetrating work of relating these affirmations to life on the housing estate and on the factory floor—and in the boardroom; the work carried out in the talk and thought of small groups of those genuinely looking for an answer. The biblical documents have much to contribute to each of these situations. But they need to be listened to with reflective attention, and in this listening the contributions of the specialists have a vital role. They send us back to the texts to see them more objectively in their historical contexts. They enable us to consider them (as we seldom do) as wholes. They encourage us to perceive, in the small things of choice of words and use of allusion, a more exact and apposite point in the affirmations being made. Bengel's famous saying remains valid: apply thyself wholly to the text, apply the whole

[1] *Old Testament Theology*, Oliver and Boyd, Vol. 1, 1962; Vol. 2, 1965.
[2] *The Day of the Preacher*, Mowbray, 1967.

9

matter to thyself. If Christian people can learn to do this, not on the scale of individual piety only, but seeing themselves all the time as inhabitants of the real world of a secular community, then they will discover a much greater precision in the notion of mission, and will see themselves in a fresh way as people with a truth to communicate.

An Approach to Teaching
MICHAEL KEELING

Anyone whose full-time education ended more than ten years ago
is likely to find today on going into a primary school that the
atmosphere and approach to learning have changed almost
beyond recognition; the sense of change may as yet be less great
on going into a secondary school, but here also change has begun
and its pace is increasing. This obviously raises questions for
those who are engaged in Christian education. What are the
reasons for the changes in secular education? On what principles
are they based? How far can and should these changes take place
also in the Church's educational work? These questions are
particularly urgent in work with children, because comparisons
are going to be drawn between the school and the Church, and if
the Church's methods are less effective than those used in
schools, this will affect the child's idea of the Church as an institution concerned with present day life; but it is also true that it is
in children's work that this need is now best understood—perhaps because the revolution has been going on so long. In this
chapter we shall be concerned mainly with work with adolescents
and adults, where the challenge is more recent and equally serious.

Changes in Education

Very broadly the changes that have been taking place can be
characterized by two technical terms that are now coming into
common use: the words "permissive" and "unstructured". The
term "permissive" applies to the atmosphere in the school, the
attitude of the teachers to the children, and it means in effect a
greater readiness to let children do things in their own way and
in their own time and a greater readiness to let the children

express what they really think and feel, to be themselves. If "permissive" is a complicated way of saying "tolerant", "unstructured" is perhaps a complicated way of saying "flexible": it means a way of teaching by building upon the interests of the children and by letting the teaching programme be guided as much by the children's response as by the teacher's own map of work. The term "unstructured" can also be relevant to the human relationships in a school, in the sense that in an unstructured setting the relationship "teacher–pupil" does not automatically mean that "teacher" is right and "pupil" is wrong if a difference of opinion occurs.

The objection that people tend to raise at this point is that this may be all very pleasant in theory, but what about the actual learning? We can best answer this by making two points about the learning process.

1. Learning is not a process that is imposed upon us, but is something that we do for ourselves: that is to say, in practice we get a firm grasp of some piece of information mainly when we become interested in it and *want* to learn about it. Compare, for example, the fund of information any adolescent has about the members of pop groups and the records they have made with the information the same adolescent has about the industrial revolution or the exports of Canada, and compare the information many adult males have about the workings of a car engine with the information the same adults have about the history of France or the membership of the British cabinet. It is in any case a mistake to regard the educational process as primarily a matter of imparting information. No one retains more than a very small part of the information which he handles during his years of full-time education (this, incidentally, puts in question the content of a good deal of Sunday School and Confirmation teaching). What education should be doing is stimulating children—and adults— to want to explore a subject and helping them to go about it. For

this reason the most effective way of educating is to build on existing interests: for example, a boy who fancies himself as a nuclear physicist will tend to be more easily interested in mathematics than in geography, and will be more interested in mathematics if he can be led to see that it is connected with nuclear physics than if it is presented to him as an entirely separate subject. Similarly, it is an important part of teaching technique to start from something that is within the experience of an individual or group and to work from that to the point which you wish to make—so that, for example, a discussion on morals might start from the words of a current song.

A correlative of this point is that we tend to learn better by finding out for ourselves than by being told: for example, children can grasp the concepts of cubic capacity more quickly by taking jugs and water and experimenting with them than by doing sums about jugs and water. Obviously the application of this principle is limited by time and by available equipment. Its equivalent in moral teaching is the free discussion of a point without being told by the teacher or leader what the "right" answer is, or even if there is one.

2. Learning is often stimulated by working together with others: children can often help each other to learn, and it is not always the "bright" child who helps the "dull" child but in various circumstances each has something to contribute to the other. It is ironical and sad that part of this process has been conventionally condemned in schools as "copying"!

There is a third point which is something of an aside in regard to the argument of this chapter, but which is worth putting in as being important in itself. This is that we learn better by being encouraged than by what psychologists call "negative reinforcement" such as reprimands or punishment. This is a strictly practical proposition, but there would be something very odd about a God-created world in which this were not true. In the

argument about comprehensive schools one of the most important considerations is the fact that selection (at eleven-plus or any
other age) constitutes a strong discouragement to those who are
not selected. The discouragement of half our children implicit in
the whole concept of "grammar" and "secondary modern"
schools has tended to be overcome in the early comprehensive
schools: in an experimental study first published in 1961,
T. W. G. Miller reported:

> In the comprehensive school, "grammar" type boys and "secondary
> modern" type boys were equally happy about the school they were
> attending and the interest and value of its courses; they also agreed
> about its standing in the community. Concerning these matters, too,
> there was a similarity in the views of the comprehensive and the
> grammar school boys. On the other hand, the boys in the secondary
> modern schools, compared with those in grammar schools, thought
> less highly of their school, its courses and its standing in the
> community".[1]

Two of the great advantages the Church has in its own teaching
work are the tradition of the mixed-ability group and the tradition of a non-punitive, voluntary approach to teaching.

This is only a brief account of two major ideas that have
emerged from specialized educational studies; the rest of this
chapter is an attempt to relate, very crudely, these two advances
in educational attitudes and methods to the job of a Christian
leader in a parish or other setting.

A Matter of Attitudes

One of the appendixes of the Plowden Report on "Children and
their Primary Schools" indicated that

> the effects of teachers' beliefs and attitudes are to be looked for not
> so much perhaps in differences in formal attainments as in children's
> beliefs and feelings about themselves and their underlying attitudes

[1] Oliver & Boyd, for the University of Birmingham Institute of Education,
London, 1965, pp. 90-1.

to school and what it stands for . . . A mere change in organization—
the abandonment of streaming, for example—unaccompanied by a
serious attempt to change teachers' attitudes, beliefs, and methods of
teaching, is unlikely to make much difference either to attainments
or—though this is less certainly based on the present evidence—to
the quality of teacher-pupil relationships.[1]

What is true of the school is true also of work in the parish, that
the first job is to get right the fundamental relationships. In the
parish this means looking at three things: the relationship between the leader and the group; the way the leader and the
group think about their sources of authority in the Bible and the
Church; and the way the leader thinks of his own job in relation
to "the Faith".

The attitude of the leader to his group—and of the group to
the leader—must be one of freedom and mutual respect. This
may seem to be a truism, but many conscientious and sincere
attempts at teaching fail because the leader has not grasped what
the nature of the teaching operation is. In the discussion of
authority in Chapter 4 the point was made that effective leadership needs to be humble, open to question, and accepting. In
practice in a group this means that every opinion offered must be
listened to and treated as valid, and that the opinions of the leader
are to be treated as no more than the opinions of one member of
the group—perhaps with more weight because of whatever
training the leader may have received, but not being taken necessarily as the "right" answer. This basis is essential if every
member is to make his own proper contribution and not either
defer to and reproduce the opinions (or what are expected to be
the opinions) of the leader, or just keep quiet. There is no method,
however good, that will work for a teacher or leader who has the

[1] Preliminary Report from the National Foundation for Educational Re-
search on the organization of junior schools and the effects of streaming.
Children and their Primary Schools, Vol. 2, Research and Surveys, p. 558,
H.M.S.O., 1967.

wrong attitude to what he is doing. On the other hand, the teacher or leader who understands the sort of attitude within the group that will open the minds of the members will succeed in teaching, whatever methods he uses. It needs to be borne in mind also that while the "institutional" leadership may rest with one appointed leader through all the meetings of a group, "moral" leadership passes from person to person according to the needs of the moment and the abilities available, so that there will be substantial periods when the designated leader is not leading in practice. The ability to recognize this when it happens is an important qualification for any official leader of a group.

Next in importance is the attitude of the group and the leader to their sources in the Bible and the Church. It is not sufficient for us just to say that something is "in the Bible": it is not sufficient for our own use and it is not sufficient as a basis from which to teach. We need to know also whether the point the Bible makes is reasonable and whether it is likely to work in our own lives. The whole strength of the Bible is that it is reasonable and that it does work—if we are afraid to let these questions be asked of it, we surely indicate that our own trust in the Bible is not great enough. We also have to be honest about what sort of material the Bible is. Not all of it is scientifically true, not all of it was written, or spoken, by the people it claims to be written or spoken by. Not all of the Bible is of equal spiritual and moral value, and some of the statements it makes contradict one another: that is to say, they involve real and not apparent contradictions. Yet, in spite of all this, more than 100 years of intense, intelligent, and not always friendly criticism of the Bible have left the foundations of the Christian faith unshaken; it is the fear of criticism rather than the practice of it that will harm the Bible. Similarly, the pronouncements of the Church have to be judged by the same test: do they work? For if they do not work we might as well shut up shop straight away. There are many matters on which there is a wide consensus of teaching in the

Christian Church, and such a consensus obviously carries great weight with those who are already strongly attached to the Church, but it does not carry weight with those who are only loosely attached or not attached at all. All doctrinal statements have practical implications in the long run, which is what makes them important; in most situations if we cannot commend them in practical terms we had better keep quiet about them.

This brings us to the question of the attitude of the leader or teacher to "the Faith" or "the Gospel". The Christian faith is not mathematics or physics; it involves an act of belief. There is, therefore, a natural tendency for the Christian leader to have a personal involvement in securing the same commitment from the members of his group (in school, in Confirmation training, in the adult congregation, or wherever it might be) as he himself feels. This tendency must be resisted. The Church is indeed in the world to spread the gospel, but the right way of evangelizing is built on two principles. The first is that the Christian commitment is essentially to Jesus Christ, the Word, the Saviour, the living Lord; it is not necessarily to all the beliefs or observances of the leader or of the Church. It is an open question what is the minimum of common belief and practice that makes people "Christians", but that minimum certainly cannot be equated with what any particular one of us happens to hold at a given time, nor can it necessarily be equated with what the Church holds to be the "fulness" of the faith, because even if the Church teaches without error (and not all Christians would assent to this) we still have to allow for those who are taking the first steps in the Christian faith but are not yet grown into the fulness; indeed all of us have room to grow in the faith. The second principle is that the most we can do is to give the other person the chance to choose for himself whether he will believe the gospel or not. Christian teaching is a matter of exposing options, of revealing the choices that can be made; it is not a matter of saying, "You must make this choice". As we said in Chapter 4, we have to love people enough not to mind (in a sense) whether they accept the Christian faith or not. Some may think that this is a betrayal of the faith—but it seems to me that it is rather the heart of the faith.

Working in Small Groups

If we take the two points about the learning process made above (pp. 118–120), that learning is something that we do for ourselves rather than have imposed on us, and that we tend to learn better by working together with others rather than by ourselves, we can find both of them applied in two techniques which are already of some importance in the work of Christian education. They apply to a limited extent in the method of working in small groups and to a much larger extent in the method of working without a formal programme (known technically as the "unstructured, self-programming group").

Most people by now have encountered the teaching situation in which, after some introductory presentation of the themes by a leader, those present are divided into small groups and asked to discuss a question or questions and report back (or to come back with a question to put to the speaker) and these questions or reports, when they are brought back, are written up on sheets of paper fixed to the wall and discussed by the whole group. This system was used in the national study courses "No Small Change" in 1965 for the Church of England and "The People Next Door" in 1967 for all the member Churches of the British Council of Churches.

The basic advantage of this method is that it is only in a small group that everyone present has the opportunity and the encouragement to put forward his own ideas on a subject. It is this process of sorting out our own ideas and testing them against the opinions and the experiences of others that is one of the most important parts of learning. It is through this process that we discover what we want to ask and to know more about. For adolescents, learning from each other is the most acceptable form of learning and the discussion in small groups is generally the most valued part of any training programme. In Michael Schofield's survey *The Sexual Behaviour of Young People*, 58% of the boys in the sample and 53% of the girls agreed with the statement "I learn more from friends of my own age than I can learn from my parents". Only 31% of the boys and 37% of the girls definitely disagreed with the statement.[1]

One difficulty that is sometimes felt, particularly by older people, is that some people do not always want to make a contribution in a group but prefer just to listen to someone talking; some people also are afraid of being asked to act as reporter for a group while others find this helps as an excuse not to contribute in other ways—which shows how wide a range of response a leader has to be alert to! The value of the group depends very much on the people who compose it and the length of time they are able to spend together, and on the quality of the material that is fed into the group during the sessions. The value of the whole exercise depends also on the whole groups from which the small groups are formed not being too large.

Work in small groups calls for some sensitivity to other people's feelings on the part of the leader. It is not necessary for everyone to speak every time, and if the group is functioning over several sessions the members will usually find to their surprise that the silent ones have at some point an extremely valuable contribution to make, and may then look back on previous sessions and discover that the silent person was really contributing by his or her presence even without speaking up. Every small group is an exercise in personal relations, in which we make discoveries about each other and about the way we react to each

[1] Page 120, Table 7.1, statement 10, (Longmans, Green, 1965). In the survey *Television and Religion*, 65% of those interviewed felt that the opinion of friends and workmates is more important in determining how people behave than is their religion (University of London Press, 1964. Paragraph 133).

other, and about the human value and experience of the other members of the group. This sort of work can develop our own sensitivity to other people's feelings and needs. On the other hand, it can also produce its own stresses and make considerable demands on patience and tolerance. Working in a small group can lead to a growth in self-knowledge, to an understanding of the sort of claims we make on a group and of the way we interact with others; but there can be factors which make some people refuse this self-knowledge and this is one of the reasons why some people find themselves unable to work happily in small groups. One clear implication of the small group method is that anybody engaged in Christian leadership and teaching should have some training in its use.

Self-programming Groups

The unstructured, self-programming group is a further development of small group work in which more emphasis is put on both the principles with which we began: that learning is something which you do for yourself, and that you can learn from working with others.

It is in some ways the adult equivalent of the primary school idea of finding out for yourself with jugs and water. Less commonly used, and perhaps less widely applicable, than small group work generally, it is nevertheless of considerable interest. Very simply, "unstructured" means that those responsible for organizing the meetings do not determine beforehand that the group will move from subject A to subject B to subject C in a predetermined order or at predetermined intervals; "self-programming" is the corollary of this, that the group itself decides, by the direction in which its talk moves, what subjects will be tackled and at what points in the meeting or series of meetings. Every group is of course programmed in a sense at the outset because either it is called together to discuss subjects in a certain area of human activity (such as "The Common Market" or

"Current Moral Problems"), or else it is composed of people drawn together by a common pursuit (for example, teachers, or members of a Parochial Church Council). This gives the subject some definition and the group some aim.

In a completely unstructured discussion this is all the definition and organization that takes place. From there on the group just talks. If sufficient time is available this can be enormously fruitful (though it is difficult to define "sufficient" because so much depends on the group itself, but say, for example, a residential course for a weekend or the inside of a week, or weekly non-residential sessions for a period of three, six, or twelve weeks). It takes a very long time for people to bring up their real ideas on anything and to discover what the things that trouble them really are; it takes a long time for the members of a group to decide that it is possible to trust each other enough to say what they really think and feel about the things that happen (this can be as true for a Church Council whose members have known each other and worked with each other for years as for a group called together for the first time). It takes time also for a group to work through all the ideas, observations, and principles that each member brings to it and considers to be important; but this has to be done if each member is to feel that he has made his proper contribution and if the group is to come to a genuine common mind. An agenda that takes up the whole meeting can prevent any of these processes ever taking place—which is why most Parochial Church Councils and other business groups are relatively ineffective as groups. But there are three cautions to be entered about the use of this method. The first is that a substantial period of unstructured discussion is a very demanding activity. It means drawing heavily on your own inner resources. This can present difficulties and even dangers for anyone who is more than usually insecure. The second is that this is not a way of working which satisfies everybody: those who are of a very active, practical, and non-analytic cast of mind can find that the apparent lack of practical action or decision in such meetings is a barrier to an understanding of the real advances that may have been made—advances in the knowledge of one's own place in a group and of the working and purpose of the group as a whole—and so can come away with the idea that "nothing has happened". This is a limitation on the method, but it does not invalidate it. The people who prefer practical action are vital in the life of a parish and it is important that "action groups" should be related to "ideas groups"—but it is not essential that everybody should be involved in both sorts of groups. The third caution is that some people may go away from an unstructured group feeling "nothing has happened" because they have come to the group with certain expectations that have not been fulfilled. This difficulty can sometimes be overcome by getting the members to fill in an "expectation sheet" when they first arrive; but even if the group in fact deals with all the points that have arisen in the expectation sheets, people can still come away with a sense of having been let down, because their real expectations have been something that they have been unable to put into words, or even to recognize in their conscious minds.

Probably the most generally useful form of the method is the partly structured group. The best way of explaining this is to describe what actually happened on one such course. The members were boys and girls drawn from the senior forms of schools over a wide area for a three day residential course which had been given the title "Teenage Problems". For most of the time the course was led by a team of two lay people and two clergy. At the beginning of the first session the members were asked to write down individually the topics or questions they expected to have discussed on the course. The results were then listed on wall sheets and the members asked to vote for each topic in turn as a way of establishing priorities. Three main groups of questions stood out as most important. In order they were: personal relationships, war, and race relations. (Many of the members came from areas in which this last was a live issue). The leaders had attempted to anticipate what the response of the members would be and had worked out possible questions for discussion; they were therefore ready immediately to send the members into small groups to discuss a question relating to the first group of topics. While the small groups were meeting the leaders also met to assess the response of the group so far, to anticipate the likely development of the discussion and to plan the next move. Each small group made its report on a wall sheet and these reports were discussed by the leaders with the whole group. During the ensuing break the leaders were able to come to a quick decision about the form of the next session. This way of working continued throughout the course. Half way through the course each member was asked to fill in an evaluation sheet giving an opinion about the most and least useful parts of the course so far, and stating what they would like to discuss in the rest of the time. The results of this evaluation closely matched the original order of priorities established in the first session, though there were of course wide individual variations. At the end of the course a similar evaluation sheet was used to judge the whole course. Almost every item in the course was put on the useful side by some members and on the not very useful side by others. The most common comment was that the small group discussions in which the members heard each other's ideas were the best part of the course. (This corresponds to Schofield's finding, see page 125 above.) Inevitably some members came away with the impression that what they wanted to discuss had not been discussed: the interpretation which the leaders' team placed upon this point was that these young people had probably been wanting to discuss problems which they had not in practice felt able to mention. This is a difficulty which is not easily overcome in an *ad hoc* group of this sort.

One thing that stands out from this way of working is the fact that it makes great demands on the team of leaders. The leaders have to be prepared with resource material of every kind. In the course of this three-day conference, as well as questions for discussion on each subject and the comment on the discussion, the team made use of two role plays, a duplicated Bible study, the words of a pop-song, and two five-minute talks (on figures relating to pre-marital chastity and illegitimate births, and on figures relating to immigration in this country and elsewhere). This material was used only where the course of the discussion seemed to demand it and other material was prepared and in other circumstances might have been used. The leaders also need a great deal of sensitivity to the needs of the group at every point if they are not simply to impose their own ideas of how the programme should develop. They should also be able to restrain themselves from putting in their own comment too forcibly or too quickly. At every point the question needs to be thrown back to the group until they are ready to demand interpretation and guidance from the leaders. In practice one of the comments in the evaluations of this course was that the leaders had come in too forcibly with their own views; but it was also in this course that in the discussion of pre-marital chastity one of the senior boys at last said to the leaders, "It is up to you to tell us what we should do", and it was at this point that the group was ready to listen and to learn. Finally, it need hardly be said that this sort of exercise can be conducted only by a team of leaders, because the mutual support, stimulation, and balance of evaluation that a team provides are essential to it. In practice the leaders' team found that they were also concerned with their own functioning as a group, and that a certain amount of working-through of situations was necessary here.

The experience of this particular course is not put forward in any way as a standard of such operations but simply as one example among many of the way it might go. The peculiarity of this way of working is that it is rather difficult to explain but very convincing when it is experienced.

The Role of the Leader

In any training or discussion group a certain amount of "feed-in" is necessary. "Feed-in" means simply "material to work on", and it can be factual information, a situation or role play to be worked out, a section of the Bible for study, a question for discussion, or definite comment and guidance from the leader. In a completely unstructured group the feed-in, apart from the initial move of defining the subject and calling the group together, comes from what each of the members puts in himself. In this sort of group there is no formal leader though at every point leadership is in fact being exercised by someone. In any other group some material for discussion and some comment must be provided by the leader or leaders. Emphasis has already been placed on the need for the leader to be sufficiently sensitive to the functioning of the group to know what to feed in and when. Emphasis has also been placed on the fact that at certain points in the process the group will be ready to be given definite guidance, at which points it can be highly effective, but that, if the leader attempts to impose guidance or instruction on the group at a point at which they are not ready for it, this will be ineffective and may set up a subconscious resentment (or even a conscious resentment) between the group and the leader. There are two other points that perhaps should be added on this. The first is that in traditional methods of teaching the danger is of too much feed-in. There are, for example, very few occasions on which it is effective for a leader or other member of a group to talk for more than five to ten minutes. (This fact throws doubt on the value of a great many activities, from sermons to university lectures.) The second is that in the modern methods of communication outlined in this chapter the danger is of not having enough feed-in. For example, in the Diocese of York, where "No Small Change" was followed by a similar diocesan exercise "Opportunity Unlimited", some people commented when "The People

10

Next Door" came up that they felt that their own need was for more "teaching" and particularly for more Bible study.

A specific difficulty attaches to the position of the clergyman as leader of a group. Whether we like it or not, the fact is that in the Church of England at least the presence of a clergyman tends to have an inhibiting effect on the self-expression of the group. There are historical and sociological as well as theological reasons for this. The net effect is that there tends to be an expectation in the group that the clergyman will be the man with the answers and that he can and should tell the group what to think. Until this barrier is broken down it is essential that the basic discussion work in a group should take place in the absence of the clergyman-leader. The same difficulty exists for any group in which there is some expectation of authority connected with the leader, whether he is a clergyman or a layman. It is true, for example, of a group of adolescents with an adult leader. In the residential course described earlier, the team of leaders did not take part in the small group discussion, although one member of the team was usually around during these meetings so that he or she could be called in by any small group that wanted help. Many clergy and many lay people find this point difficult to accept, but it seems to be confirmed by the experience of most people who have tried these methods of working.

Conclusion

The common thread running through all that we have said in this chapter and in chapter 4 is respect for the individual human being. In terms of teaching method this respect justifies itself by its effectiveness. The two techniques we have discussed in detail— the small group and the self-programming group—are based on an approach to the individual which assumes that he is of sufficient importance in the sight of God for his ideas and his way of doing things to be of major importance in the way we deal with him. These techniques are also important because they work.

Some people are alarmed at the idea of setting people free to discuss and to question and to disagree, fearing perhaps that in conditions of freedom people will not really want to know about the love of God. All one can say in reply to this is that the experience of those who have tried these methods has been the exact opposite: that, when people are set free to say what they really think and feel about matters of importance, sooner or later they want to know what the Christian faith says about these matters, and then they really are open to the gospel (which is not to say, of course, that they all then accept what the gospel says— but neither did the people in Athens and elsewhere when Paul talked to them). Certainly these methods are more difficult to handle for both sides than a forty minute talk from the vicar or whoever, but they can also be vastly more rewarding for both sides.

There is at the present time a much more vivid awareness of the value of the individual human being and of the importance of freedom in the life of the individual than has existed at any time previously in the history of western Europe. This is true both in religious and in secular activities. Obviously there are entries to be made on the debit side, but overall there is an impression of a movement of the Spirit in human life which is far-reaching and hopeful. In this chapter we have looked only at some details of educational attitudes and methods, but it is through such details that the Spirit works, and what we have been talking about here is, I believe, an advance in the understanding of Christian mission itself.

NOTE

A more detailed discussion of the principles of inductive training methods can be found in *Learning to Live* by David Manship, published by Pergamon Press; some actual training situations are discussed in the *Trainers in Action* series of pamphlets published by the Church Information Office; Confirmation training material based on the principles discussed in this chapter is published by the Bible Reading Fellowship in their *Confirmation and After* series of courses.

Willingly to School
GORDON HOPKINS

Secularism: Gain and Loss

The kind of person who likes, stridently, to pronounce in the round about the relationship between active Christians and the whole world of education would soon be found out, because, today, there are so many cross currents, contradictory encounters, and unexpected meeting points.

Inter-denominational battles no longer flare up; so that educationalists are less likely to will "a plague on both your houses". The struggle to maintain the dual system has taken on a different hue. The Anglican can no longer attempt to compete with the State (except perhaps still in Lancashire), but is anxious effectively to keep a stake in the field, and to make sure that any new building is well planned and staffed, and is ready to make a significant contribution in the field of religious education.

The enmity between clergy and teachers was pretty widespread twenty-five years ago, and quite often had something of the same flavour as the feud between the _curé_ and the schoolmaster in France. This was largely due to the way in which the Anglican vicar had lorded it over the schoolmaster in rural and some urban areas. That kind of social domination has, since the war, gone from the Anglican clergy for ever. Equally, school teachers have gradually lost a good deal of their authority. In spite of the affluent society, they are teaching today against a background of social and domestic disintegration. In the north of England a great many school teachers are ready and willing to co-operate with the clergy in tackling very many problems which they face jointly. In London and the Home Counties the secularist wind is a good deal more cutting. In the provinces, if the clergy are prepared to mind their step and to be of use, they can very often serve teachers and children in provided schools in ways which go deeper than merely allowing the church to be used for harvest and carol services.

Of course, secularism is far more overt and militant within the whole field of higher education. The modern "Lucky Jim" is a more dubious character than the agnostic of the Shaw, Wells, Huxley era. More pathetic is the failed "Lucky Jim", who ends up in purveying Liberal Studies, which no one takes seriously, at one level or another in a technical or technological college. The toughest assignment a priest can face is that of being chaplain in a modern secular university.

Religious Education: an Assessment

Back in the parish, however, the Vicar sends some of the more promising youngsters to a Deanery Youth Week-end Conference. Inevitably, during group discussions, there rises the lament and refrain about the religious instruction which they receive in school. Some of this can be discounted, because young people enjoy shocking the party, but it does add up to an indictment of a good deal that goes on in secondary and grammar schools under the heading of R.E. However, there are dangers over pontificating at this point. There is a substantial amount of sound work done in R.E. in secondary and grammar schools, but it goes unsung. It would be folly for the more oncoming clergy at this point to jump on to the secularist band-waggon, with the aim of putting a stop to R.E. If this was done, the clergy would be ignoring the genuinely fine and devoted work done by large numbers of devoted Christian teachers in provided primary schools. But for this work a large percentage of English children would be as ignorant of the Christian faith as are their brothers in the islands of the South Seas. The situation is hard to assess. It would be wrong to be either optimistic or aggressively pessimistic. On the whole, in these days, the greater danger is for the clergy to lament overmuch that "they have thrown down thine altars and slain the prophets with the sword, and I, even I, only, am left" (1 Kings 19). Even if that were true, it is better to get to grips with an intractable job in an awkward situation instead of protesting overmuch.

Opportunities for the Parish Priest

Soon after the last war an interesting situation arose when the present writer became aware of a large number of the lads in the parish who were "packing in their night schools". This was serious because, at the time, nearly all the apprentices embarked on the preliminary course, leading first to Ordinary, and then to Higher National Certificate, and a great many of them were no-where near that kind of calibre; and when they came down at the preliminaries that ended their further education. A friend of the Ministry of Education at Curzon Street gave some excellent advice, the H.M.I. for Technical Education became actively interested, and so did the Assistant Director for the Local Authority. They all came to a meeting in the Vicarage, with some of the leading industrialists, and had a good look at the whole question. It was not very long before a good many alternative craft courses were made available for the ordinary run-of-the-mill apprentices. Most of these were City and Guild courses.

For some time now, of course, the young worker has had further education in every case, a great many through day release, others through preliminary courses of a year or more at the College of Further Education before going to their firm's works.

Service on the Youth Employment Sub-committee of the Education Committee is especially interesting and worthwhile. The work of Youth Employment Officers is a most essential social service, which depends on people of enthusiasm and devotion, but their work is often little recognized, and they are still underpaid.

In 1962, owing to a sudden crisis, we were faced in Sunderland, at the height of the "bulge", with a very large number of school-leavers, and very few openings indeed in the local industries for young workers. *The Times* gave some prominence to a full letter which came to them from the Vicarage at St Luke's, Pallion. This brought in a good deal of correspondence to the writer from people who were genuinely concerned. At the same time other people who were officially involved came up from London, and were anxious to give every possible help to the Youth Employment Officer. For a year or more things were difficult, and then, more quickly than had been expected, the whole employment situation eased a good deal locally. At the time it was interesting to note that it was much easier to find work for girls in factories than to find work for boys leaving school.

These two instances have been given to show how a parish priest was able to get in touch effectively with well established social and educational agencies, who were then able to proceed, in co-operation with other interested persons, in fulfilling their own function within the community. A parish priest can get in touch with people and can put them in possession of facts and situations as and when they arise. If he is sensible he will do this unobtrusively, and will not be anxious for kudos to accrue to himself as a person, or to the Church as an institution. The parish priest can carry through some worthwhile projects by using initiative and imagination, but he would not be in a position to do so if he were himself a professional social worker; and those who hanker after that kind of role must be credited with zeal, but it is not always according to knowledge!

Teaching Deprived Children

Earlier on reference was made to the fact that those who have been teaching all their lives are very conscious of the fact that their work is done amongst children who present them today with more social problems than was ever the case in the past. At first many people may be surprised to hear this, because in the past it was widely expected that, when people had more money, social conditions would automatically improve. The deterioration is attributed by the teachers to the fact that both parents now, almost universally, go out to work, and partly to a pretty widespread failure on the part of a great many parents to establish any viable relationship, at any significant level at all, with their own children. In a great many cases they fob off their own children with cash, and then feel free to neglect them emotionally.

Today, in a good many large industrial towns in the north of England, there are an alarming number of young people who are socially deprived and who look tragically rejected. Some of them are in small pockets within the new estates, and some in problem areas. It may be, in these days of wider opportunities, that the less able feel more explicitly rejected than ever before. An observer can have the curious sensation of standing at the foot of a moving staircase, watching the able people go up and the less able, somewhat pathetically, going down on the other side.

In industrial areas there seems to be a large number of boys and girls who are not in the educationally sub-normal category, but are of a noticeably poor academic potential. Many of these children really need teaching by the kind of dedicated man or woman who teaches in E.S.N. schools. Such teachers might well be suitably rewarded, in the hope that this would end the fearful rate of mobility which bedevils the work in so many schools, to the great detriment of the children. The work is permanently demanding upon teachers, and it is not fair on them to expect them to work miracles with children who come from social backgrounds which, in many respects, have been deteriorating in recent years. Of course, a teacher will wish to test and develop the capacities of the children to their fullest extent, but they cannot inject intellectual capacities into those who do not possess them. Sometimes parents expect this of them because they are unable to face the fact that their child does not have an academic bent and must be trained along different lines.

The Church and the Comprehensive School

Educationists are, of course, very hopeful that some at least of these problems can be tackled effectively in comprehensive schools. In fact it might well be said that the very existence of these problems, which were high-lighted in the Newsom Report, are a large part of the *raison d'être* for comprehensive schools. It is unfortunate that the question of comprehensive education became bedevilled by party politics, because the issues are too complex, and too important educationally, to allow them to be obscured in this way.

The very general demand for equality of opportunity caused a much larger proportion of English children to be admitted to selective schools during the last twenty-five years. Yet the education provided in grammar schools has traditionally been severely academic in type, designed for children who are reasonably able intellectually, and it is judged by the number of pupils who gain places at the universities. In recent years the intake has included a disturbingly large number of children who do not respond to the kind of education that is designed for academically inclined people, and too many of these have lost their way and ended up with a sense of failure. Meanwhile, the gifted sixth-formers have done well, gone to the university, and embarked with promise on excellent careers.

Since, during those years, such a large number of children went to selective schools, the secondary modern school, in many difficult districts in industrial areas, were left with boys and girls who had "failed the eleven-plus". From the age of eleven to fifteen they had to continue their formal education, often in old buildings, often with some sense of rejection. These children, the "heroes" of the Newsom Report, found the familiar academic round increasingly uncongenial, and they tended to become rebellious and a real problem to their teachers, especially in their last year at school in difficult areas in industrial towns.

It is essential to ensure that the staffing of comprehensive schools achieves a genuine nexus between staff and pupils at various levels, so that boys and girls know that they are accountable to their housemaster or mistress, and/or, to the member of the staff who functions as "moral tutor". The Head needs to be an able administrator, and to work happily through a large staff. If a staff is contented and fulfilled, in work that is responsible and rewarding, there ought to be some hope that the excessive staff mobility, which has in recent years dogged the work of the schools, may be checked.

Some comprehensive schools have well-staffed departments for religious education, and, with the large resources at their disposal, they are able to embark on extremely interesting and worthwhile local projects and surveys.

One of the curious cross-currents and unexpected meeting points today, in the whole field of Christian education, is the fact that a great many more young people than for a long time have received some technical training in Old and New Testament studies. A good many more boys and girls take the R.E. papers at O-level, others at O- and A-level. Some of these go on to read Theology at the university. A large number of these are women who go back into teaching R.E. in schools. A very large number of young men and women encounter the subject and the problem in Colleges of Education, and now that the course in all these colleges is for three years students will, in quite a number of cases, gain a fairly full knowledge of the subject. This can be happening in all Colleges of Education, and not only the Church Colleges. On the whole, it is still true that much larger numbers of school teachers go to their parish church than do members of any other profession. In addition, there are more clergy than there used to be who are employed teaching R.E. in the Local Authority schools. Some of them do this extremely well. Education Committees should, however, keep a weather-eye open for the cleric who has lost his faith, and applies to teach R.E. in a Local Authority school. He may have a degree in Theology, and on those but no other grounds be eligible.

A well-staffed R.E. department in a comprehensive school does provide a very worthwhile opportunity for friendly dialogue between the school and the parochial clergy of all denominations.

The local Church should take account of the fact that many more men and women have had some advanced theological training in two ways. First, in seeking to benefit from their specialist knowledge, and, secondly, in bearing in mind the fact that educated and knowledgeable men and women will not in the future be content with a somewhat thin theological diet from parochial pulpits.

The Service of Youth

In every area the Service of Youth comes under the umbrella of the Further Education Sub-committee. The Local Authority is served by a Youth Organizer, who has always co-operated with the voluntary youth organizations. Much the largest sponsoring body of these is the Church of England. It is probable that, in the future, Local Authorities will provide more Youth Centres. Where this is done there will be less need for the Church to sponsor open youth work, but a greater need for clergy and youth leaders to co-operate in the work that is being done in locally provided Youth Centres. Of course there will always be a need for the Church to do sound educational work amongst its own professing members. Christians visiting this country from the continent are amazed that so much Anglican youth work seeks to entertain young people, whereas on the continent very much more work of an educational sort is done, and some of this is demanding in time and effort from the young people, and, as a result, they tend to be more appreciative of it.

As a result of the Albemarle Report, the Church of England in a great many areas embarked, through substantial grant aid, on the building of large Youth Centres. In de-Christianized urban areas these centres seem to be the only possible point of contact with older boys and girls. Later on, however, difficulties arose over staffing and maintenance of such large premises by the Church. It is questionable whether very much worthwhile work can be done through such centres in leading young people to any real understanding of the Christian faith.

Undoubtedly the Church must be outward rather than inward looking; but, the question remains as to the best use of time, plant, and resources by the Church in the field of Youth work. On the face of it, it looks as though the clergy would be better employed in coping in some depth with the religious education of committed Church people on the one hand, and in a willingness to make and keep informal contact with Local Authority, and other, Open Youth Clubs, but without being involved in the direct labour of providing premises and programmes.

An enormous amount of devoted work was done voluntarily in the past by Church people in and through youth organizations of all sorts and descriptions. Today this is being done increasingly by trained, paid youth workers. Some of these do the work with great competence and with a pretty clear sense of vocation; yet the fact remains that some others who man the jobs in full-time youth work have a less satisfactory professional attitude to the job, and some of them very quickly develop a curious sort of *malaise* which looks rather like a Cinderella complex. In theory there is everything to be said for trained salaried workers, but in practice they very often lack the kind of *élan* which enables a man or woman to achieve worthwhile results with young people.

Nursery Schools and Community Associations, with their work among old age pensioners, are both serviced by Education Authorities; so that their scope involves people today from the cradle to the grave. There are endless points of contact at which a Christian ministry can be of use. At whatever point co-operation is possible it becomes increasingly necessary for it to be effected unobtrusively and without any desire to boost the Church as an institution.

Clergy and educationalists ought to be able to get on well together. Both are trying professionally to tackle vast and intractable problems, both are unreasonably expected to have all the answers, and neither ought ever to expect life to be plain sailing for very long at a stretch. Yet in the midst of all the stresses and strains both expect some solid fulfilment through their work.